DATE DUE

AP 10 '0			
OC 15 '04			
NO 29 '04			

DEMCO 38-296

STEPHEN HAWKING

STEPHEN HAWKING

Quest for a Theory of the Universe

by Kitty Ferguson

Franklin Watts
New York/London/Toronto/Sydney
1991

: Nebula in Orion
vife Jane, and sons, Robert, left,
eceived an Honorary Doctor of
....nbridge University

Diagrams by Vantage Art.

Photographs copyright ©: MMP Cambridge/Melvyn Sibson: p. 2;
Washington Post Writers Group/Berke Breathed: p. 25. Insert
photographs copyright ©: Stephen Hawking: pp. 1, 2, 3, 5, 6, 8;
Y. Ferguson: p. 4 top; Gillman & Soame: p. 4 bottom; Woodfin
Camp & Associates, Inc.: pp. 9 (Julian Calder), 10 (Homer Sykes);
Stephen Shames/Visions: pp. 11, 13 bottom, 16; Miriam Berkley: pp.
12, 13 top; James Diggle, orator: p. 14; AP/Wide World Photos: p. 15.

Figure 7-9 appears courtesy of John Wheeler. Figure 9-1 courtesy
of Andrew Dunn

Library of Congress Cataloging-in-Publication Data

Ferguson, Kitty.
Stephen Hawking : quest for a theory of the universe / by Kitty
Ferguson.
p.   cm.
Includes bibliographical references and index.
Summary: Presents the life of the British theoretical physicist
who has taken the study of cosmology farther than most in his field,
despite the need for a wheelchair and computer in order to travel
and communicate.
ISBN 0-531-11067-2
1. Hawking, S. W. (Stephen W.)—Biography—Juvenile literature.
2. Cosmology—Juvenile literature.   3. Physicists—Great Britain—
Biography—Juvenile literature.   [1. Hawking, S. W. (Stephen W.)
2. Physicists.   3. Physically handicapped.   4. Cosmology.]
I. Title.
QC16.H33F47   1991
530.1—dc20   91-15956   CIP   AC

Contents

To Yale

The author wishes to thank Stephen Hawking
for his time and patience
in helping her understand his theories.

She is also grateful to the following
for their help, and for reading and checking over
portions of this book:

Larry F. Abbott, James Bardeen, Sidney Coleman,
Paul Davies, Bryce DeWitt,
Yale Ferguson, Matthew Fremont, Don Page,
Joanna Sanferrare, Herman Vetter and Tina Vetter,
and John A. Wheeler

Nonetheless, any shortcomings in this book are the
author's full responsibility.

"The greatest quest
in all science."

In Cambridge, England, there is an old narrow street called Free School Lane. It begins by the eleventh-century church of St. Bene't's, bends past bicycles tethered to the churchyard fence and flowers and branches that droop through the iron palings, and then widens beside a wall of black, rough stones with slitlike windows, the back of fourteenth-century Corpus Christi College. Nearby, across the lane, a plaque beside a Gothic-style gateway reads, THE CAVENDISH LABORATORY.

Other gateways in Cambridge lead to very old and splendid courtyards. The courtyard beyond the gateway of the "Old Cavendish" isn't like those. There's nothing left of the friary that stood here in the twelfth century or the gardens that later grew on its ruins. Instead, there are gray asphalt pavement and factorylike buildings, almost bleak enough to be a prison. Nevertheless, for a century, until Cambridge University built the "New" Cavendish Labs in 1974, this was one of the most important centers of physics research in the world. In these buildings, "J.J." Thomson discovered the electron,

9

Ernest Rutherford probed the structure of the atom—and the list goes on and on.

In the Cockcroft Lecture Room here, on April 29, 1980, scientists and university dignitaries gathered in steep tiers of seats, facing a two-story wall of chalkboard and slide screen. The occasion was the inaugural lecture of a new Lucasian Professor of Mathematics, the thirty-eight-year-old mathematician and physicist Stephen William Hawking.

The title of the lecture was a question: "Is the End in Sight for Theoretical Physics?" and Hawking startled his listeners by announcing that he thought it was. He invited them to join him in a sensational escape through time and space to find the Holy Grail of science: the theory that explains the universe and everything that happens in it.

Stephen Hawking sat silently in a wheelchair while one of his students read his lecture for the assembled company. Judged on appearance alone, Hawking didn't seem a promising choice to lead any adventure. Theoretical physics is for him the great escape from a prison much more grim than any suggested by the Old Cavendish Labs. Since his early twenties he's lived with increasing disability and the promise of an early death. Hawking has amyotrophic lateral sclerosis, known in America as Lou Gehrig's disease after the Yankee first baseman who died of it. The progress of the disease in Hawking's case has been slow, but by the time he became Lucasian Professor he could no longer walk, write, feed himself, or raise his head if it tipped forward. His speech was slurred and almost unintelligible except to those who knew him best. For the Lucasian lecture, he had painstakingly dictated his text earlier, so that it could be read by the student. But Hawking was and is no invalid. He is an active, brilliant mathematician and physicist, whom some have called the most brilliant since Einstein. The Lucasian Professorship is an illustrious position once held by Sir Isaac Newton.

10

It was typical Hawking audacity to begin this distinguished professorship by predicting the end of his own field. He said he thought there was a good chance the so-called Theory of Everything would be found before the close of the century, leaving little for theoretical physicists like himself to do.

Since that lecture, many people have come to think of Stephen Hawking as the standard-bearer of the quest for a theory to explain the universe. However, the candidate he named for Theory of Everything was not one of his own theories but "N = 8 Supergravity," a theory which many physicists hoped might unify all the particles and the forces of nature. Hawking is quick to point out that his work is only one part of a much larger picture, involving physicists all over the world, and also part of a very old picture: The longing to understand the universe is almost as ancient as human consciousness. Ever since we first noticed there is pattern in nature, we've been trying to explain it with myths, religion, and later mathematics and science. We may not be much nearer to understanding the complete pattern than our remotest ancestors, but most of us like to think, with Stephen Hawking, that we are.

Stephen Hawking says he doesn't want anyone to write a biography of him, and though this book will tell you a great deal about his life and about him as a person, it is certainly not a biography in the usual sense. In fact, you wouldn't learn very much about Hawking from a "biography." In order to understand him at all you have to find out at least a little about his science and share his excitement in it. When I interviewed him in December 1989 and June 1990, we spent most of our time talking about the scientific side of the book. This *science* is what *he* would like you to know about him.

This is a book full of paradoxes. In science and with people, things are often not what they seem, and pieces that ought to fit together refuse to do so. You'll learn that beginnings may be endings; cruel circumstances can lead to happiness, although fame and success may not; two great scientific theories taken together seem to give us nonsense; empty space isn't empty; black holes aren't black; and a man whose appearance inspires shock and pity takes us laughing to where the boundaries of time and space ought to be—but are not.

Anywhere we look in our universe, we find that reality is amazingly complex and elusive, sometimes alien, not always easy to take, impossible to predict. Can any scientific theory truly explain it *all*?

2

"Our goal is nothing less than a complete description of the universe we live in."

Imagine you have never seen our universe. Is there a set of rules so complete that by studying them you could discover exactly what our universe is like? Could you read through those rules in a lifetime? Many physicists believe it would take you much less time than that. They think the rule book is short and that it contains a set of fairly simple principles, perhaps even just one principle that lies behind everything that has happened, is happening, and ever will happen in our universe. Stephen Hawking says that set of rules—that Theory of Everything—may be within our reach.

Archaeologists digging in the ruins of the ancient city of Ur in Mesopotamia unearthed an exquisite inlaid board with a few small carved pieces. It's obviously an elaborate game, but we know nothing of the rules by which it was played. We can only deduce them from the design of the board and the pieces.

The universe is something like that: a magnificent,

elegant, mysterious game. Clearly there are rules, but we haven't been supplied with a rule book. However, the universe is no beautiful, dead relic like the game found at Ur. The game of the universe continues. We and everything we know about (and much we do not) are in the thick of the play. If there is a Theory of Everything, we and everything in the universe must be obeying its principles, even while we try to discover what they are.

You might expect the complete, unabridged rules for the universe to fill a vast library. There would be rules for how celestial bodies form and move, for how human bodies work and stop working, for how humans relate to one another, for how subatomic particles interact, how water freezes, how trees grow, how dogs bark—intricate rules within rules within rules. How could all of that possibly be reduced to a few principles?

The fact is that science has for centuries been finding that nature is often less complicated than it first appears. The idea that all of it may come down to something remarkably simple isn't new or farfetched.

Richard Feynman, the American physicist and Nobel prize winner, gives us an introduction to the way the process works. He reminds us that there was a time when we had something we called motion and something else called heat and something else again called sound. "But it was soon discovered," writes Feynman, "after Sir Isaac Newton explained the laws of motion, that some of these apparently different things were aspects of the same thing. For example, the phenomena of sound could be completely understood as the motion of atoms in the air. So sound was no longer considered something in addition to motion. It was also discovered that heat phenomena are easily understandable from the laws of motion. In this way, great globs of physics theory were synthesized into a simplified theory."[1]

The Rules behind the Rules

All matter as we normally think of it in the universe—people, air, ice, stars, gases, microbes, this book—is made up of tiny building blocks called atoms. Atoms in turn are made up of smaller objects, called particles, and a lot of empty space. Some of the particles are made up of even smaller particles.

The most familiar matter particles are the protons and neutrons in the nuclei of atoms, and the electrons that orbit the nuclei. Matter particles (which belong to a class of particles called **fermions**) have a system of messages that pass among them, causing them to act and change in certain ways. A group of humans might have a message system consisting of four different services: telephone, fax, mail, and carrier pigeon. Not all the humans would send and receive messages and influence one another by means of all four services. If you think of the message system among the fermions as four such services, which we call **forces,** you won't be far wrong. There are other particles that carry these messages among the fermions, and sometimes among themselves as well: "messenger" particles, more properly called **bosons.** Every particle in the universe is either a fermion or a boson.

One of the four forces is **gravity.** You can think of the gravitational force holding you to the earth as "messages" carried by bosons called **gravitons** between the particles of the atoms in your body and the particles of the atoms in the earth, telling these particles to draw closer to one another. A second force, the **electromagnetic force,** is messages carried by bosons called **photons** between the protons in the nucleus of an atom and the electrons nearby, and among electrons. It causes electrons to orbit the nucleus. On our level, much larger than atoms, photons show up as light. A third message

15

service, the **strong force,** causes the nucleus of the atom to hold together. A fourth, the **weak force,** causes radioactivity.

The activities of the four forces are responsible for all messages among all fermions in the universe and for all interactions among them. Without the four forces, every fermion (every particle of matter) would exist, if it existed at all, in isolation, with no means of contacting or influencing any other, oblivious to every other. To put it bluntly, whatever *doesn't* happen by means of one of the four forces doesn't happen. A complete understanding of the forces would give us an understanding of the principles underlying everything that happens in the universe. Already we have a remarkably condensed rule book.

Much of the work of physicists in this century has been aimed at learning more about how the four forces of nature operate and how they're related. In our human message system, we might discover that telephone and fax are not two separate services, but the same thing showing up in two different ways. That discovery would "unify" the two message services. In a similar way, physicists have sought, with some success, to unify the forces. They hope ultimately to find a theory which explains all four forces as one "superforce" showing up in different ways and also unites both fermions and bosons in a single family. They speak of such a theory as a unified theory.

A theory explaining the universe, the Theory of Everything, must go a step further and answer the question, What was the universe like at the instant of beginning, before any time whatsoever had passed? Physicists phrase that question, What are the "initial conditions" or the "boundary conditions at the beginning of the universe"? ("Boundary conditions" can also mean the conditions at any "edge" of the universe: the end of the universe, for example, or the center of a black hole.) A complete understanding of the "superforce" may give us an understanding of the boundary conditions. Or it may be that we need to know the boundary conditions before we can understand the superforce. The two are inextricably linked. Theorists are working their way toward a Theory of Everything from both directions.

Language Lesson

There are a few terms you need to know before we go on. First, when scientists use the word *predict*, they don't mean telling the future. The question, Does this theory predict the speed of light? isn't asking whether the theory tells us what that speed will be next Tuesday. It means, Would this theory make it possible for us to figure out the speed of light if we couldn't observe what that speed is?

Let's also be certain about the meaning of the word *theory*. A theory is not Truth with a capital *T*, not a rule, not fact, not the final word. You might think of a theory as a toy boat. To find out whether it floats, you set it on the water. You test it. When it sinks, you build a different boat.

Some theories are good boats. They float a long time. We may know there are a few leaks, but for all practical purposes they serve us well. Some serve us so well, and are so solidly supported by experiment and testing, that we begin to regard them as truth. Scientists, remembering how complex and surprising our universe is, are extremely wary about calling them that. Although some theories do have a lot of experimental success to back them up and others are hardly more than a glimmer in a theorist's eyes—brilliantly designed boats that have never been tried on the water—it's a

17

mistake to assume that any of them is absolute scientific "truth."

In *A Brief History of Time* Stephen Hawking tells us a scientific theory is "just a model of the universe, or a restricted part of it, and a set of rules that relate quantities in the model to observations that we make. It exists only in our minds and does not have any other reality (whatever that may mean)."[2] The easiest way to understand this definition is to use some examples.

When Hawking has his assistant set a cardboard cylinder on the seminar table and tells his students, "Now it just so happens that we have the universe here," he's showing them a model of the universe. A "model," of course, doesn't have to be something like a cardboard cylinder or a drawing that we can see and touch. It can be a mental picture or even a story. Mathematical equations or creation myths can be models.

Getting back to the cardboard cylinder, how does it resemble the universe? To make a full-fledged theory out of it, he must explain how the model is related to what we actually see around us, to "observations," or to what we might observe if we had better technology. However, just because someone sets a piece of cardboard on the table and tells how it's related to the actual universe doesn't mean anyone should accept this as *the* model of the universe. We're to consider it, not swallow it hook, line, and sinker. It's an idea, existing "only in our minds." The cardboard cylinder may turn out to be an accurate model. On the other hand, some evidence may turn up to prove that it isn't. We'll have found that we're part of a slightly different game from the one the model suggested we were playing. Would that mean the theory was "bad"? No, it may have been a very good theory, and everyone may have learned a great deal from considering it, testing it, and having to change it or discard it. It may lead to something more accurate.

What is it then that makes a theory a good theory?

Quoting Hawking again, it must "accurately describe a large class of observations on the basis of a model that contains only a few arbitrary elements, and it must make definite predictions about the results of future observations."[3]

For example, Isaac Newton's theory of gravity describes a very large class of observations. It predicts the behavior of objects dropped or thrown on earth, as well as planetary orbits.

It's important to remember, however, that a good theory doesn't have to arise entirely from observation. A good theory can be a wild theory, a great leap of imagination. "The ability to make these intuitive leaps is really what characterizes a good theoretical physicist," says Hawking.[4] However, a good theory shouldn't be at odds with things already observed, unless it gives convincing reasons for seeming to be at odds. Superstring theory, one of the most exciting current theories, predicts ten dimensions, a prediction that certainly seems inconsistent with observation. Theorists explain the discrepancy by suggesting the extra dimensions are curled up so small we can't find them.

What does Hawking mean by "arbitrary elements"? Here's an example: You learned earlier that the electromagnetic force and the weak force are two of the four forces of nature. Physicists know the strength of each of those two forces. The electroweak theory, which unifies the two, cannot tell us how to calculate the difference in strength between the two forces. The difference in strength is an "arbitrary element," not predicted by the theory. We know what it is from observation in laboratories, and so we put it into the theory "by hand." This is considered a weakness in the theory.

You mustn't conclude from this that laboratory observation is somehow at odds with good theory. The final requirement for a good theory mentioned by Hawking is that it must tell us what to expect from future observations. It must challenge us to test it. It must tell us what we will observe if the theory is correct. It should also tell us what observations would prove that it *isn't* correct. For example, Albert Einstein's theory of general relativity predicts that beams of light from distant stars bend a certain amount as they pass massive bodies like the sun. This prediction is testable. Tests show Einstein was correct.

We should point out that some theories, including most of Stephen Hawking's, are impossible to test with our present technology. We can't observe the universe in its earliest stages to find out directly whether his "no-boundary proposal" (see Chapter 7) is correct. Although some tests have been proposed for proving or disproving "wormholes" (Chapter 9), Hawking doesn't think they'll succeed. But he's told us what he thinks we'll find if we ever do have the technology, and he is convinced that his theories are consistent with what we have observed so far.

Now that we've discussed what a scientific theory is, and what it isn't, we're ready for the question, What would a theory to explain the universe be like?

Challenges for "Theory of Everything" Candidates

• It must give us a model that unifies the forces and particles.

• It must answer the question, What are the "boundary conditions" of the universe, the conditions at the very instant of beginning, before any time whatsoever passed?

• It must allow few options. It ought to be "restrictive." It should, for instance, predict precisely how many types of particles there are. If it leaves options, it must somehow account for the fact that we have the universe we have and not a slightly different one.

• It should contain few arbitrary elements. We learned earlier what that means. Later in this book you'll find that Hawking's "wormhole" theory may mean we'll never have a theory without arbitrary elements. Nevertheless, we'd rather not have to peek too often at the actual universe for answers. Paradoxically, the Theory of Everything itself may be an arbitrary element. Few scientists expect it to explain why there should exist either a theory or anything at all for it to describe. It won't answer Stephen Hawking's question "Why does the universe go to all the bother of existing?"[5]

• It must predict a universe like the universe we observe or else explain convincingly why there's a discrepancy. If it predicts that light speed is ten miles per hour, or doesn't allow for penguins or pulsars, we have a problem. A Theory of Everything must find a way to survive comparison with what we observe.

• It should be simple, although it must allow for enormous complexity. The physicist John Archibald Wheeler of Princeton writes:

> *Behind it all*
> *is surely an idea so simple,*
> *so beautiful,*
> *so compelling that when—*
> *in a decade, a century,*
> *or a millennium—*
> *we grasp it,*
> *we will all say to each other,*
> *how could it have been otherwise?*
> *How could we have been so stupid*
> *for so long?*[6]

The most profound theories, such as Newton's theory of gravity and Einstein's relativity theories, are simple in the way Wheeler describes.

21

• It must solve the enigma of combining Einstein's theory of general relativity (a theory we use to explain gravity) with quantum mechanics (the theory we use when talking about the other three forces). This is the challenge that Stephen Hawking has taken up. We'll introduce the problem here. You'll understand it better after you've read about the uncertainty principle of quantum mechanics later in this chapter and about general relativity in Chapter 4.

Einstein's theory of general relativity is the theory of the large and the very large—stars, planets, galaxies, for instance. It does an excellent job of explaining how gravity works on that level.

Quantum mechanics is the theory that speaks of the forces of nature as messages among fermions (matter particles). Quantum mechanics also contains something extremely frustrating, the **uncertainty principle:** We can never know precisely both the *position* of a particle and its *velocity* (speed and direction) at the same time. In spite of this problem, quantum mechanics does an excellent job of explaining things on the level of the very small.

One way to combine these two great twentieth-century theories into one unified theory would be to explain gravity as an exchange of messenger particles, as we do successfully with the other three forces. Another avenue is to rethink general relativity in the light of the uncertainty principle.

When we think of gravity as an exchange of messenger particles, there are problems. We've said that you can think of the force holding you to the earth as the exchange of gravitons (messenger particles of gravity) between the matter particles in your body and the matter particles that make up the earth. When you do that, you're describing the gravitational force in a quantum-mechanical way. But because all these gravitons are also exchanging gravitons among themselves, mathematically this is messy business. We get infinities, mathematical nonsense.

Physical theories can't really handle infinities. When they've appeared in other theories, theorists have resorted to something known as "renormalization." "No matter how clever the word," wrote the physicist Richard Feynman, "it is what I would call a dippy process!"[7] Feynman had to use it when he developed a theory to explain the electromagnetic force, and he wasn't pleased about it. The process involves putting in other infinities and letting the infinities cancel each other out. It does sound suspicious, but in many cases it seems to work in practice. The resulting theories agree with observation remarkably well.

Renormalization works in the case of electromagnetism, but it fails in the case of gravity. The infinities in the gravitational force are of a much nastier breed than those in the electromagnetic force. They refuse to go away. Supergravity, the theory Hawking spoke about in his Lucasian lecture, and superstring theory, in which the basic objects in the universe are not pointlike particles but tiny strings, have made promising inroads. But the problem isn't solved yet.

On the other hand, what if we allow quantum mechanics to invade the study of the very large, the realm where gravity seems to reign supreme? What happens when we rethink what general relativity tells us about gravity in the light of what we know about the uncertainty principle, the principle that you can't measure accurately the position and the velocity of a particle at the same time? Will this make a great difference? You'll learn that Stephen Hawking's work along these lines has had bizarre results: black holes aren't black, and the boundary conditions may be that there are no boundaries.

While we're listing paradoxes, here's another:

Empty space isn't empty. Later in this book you'll see how we arrive at that conclusion. For now be content to know that the uncertainty principle means that so-called empty space teems with particles and antiparticles. (The matter-antimatter used in science fiction is a familiar example.)

At the same time general relativity tells us that the presence of matter or energy makes spacetime curve, or warp. We've already mentioned one result of that curvature: the bending of light beams from distant stars as they pass a massive body like the sun.

Keep those two points in mind: (1) "Empty" space is filled with particles and antiparticles. They add up to an enormous amount of energy—an infinite amount. (2) The presence of this energy causes curvature of spacetime.

Combining the two ideas, we must conclude that the entire universe ought to be curled up into a small ball. This hasn't happened. When general relativity and quantum mechanics work together, what they predict seems to be dead wrong. Both general relativity and quantum mechanics are exceptionally good theories, two of the outstanding intellectual achievements of the twentieth century. They serve us magnificently not only for theoretical purposes but in many practical ways. Nevertheless, put together they yield infinities and nonsense. The Theory of Everything must somehow resolve that nonsense.

Predicting the Details

Once again imagine that you've never seen our universe. With the Theory of Everything you ought nevertheless to be able to predict everything about it. It's possible you can predict suns and planets and galaxies and black holes and quasars—but can you predict next year's Kentucky Derby winner? How specific can you be? Not very.

The calculations necessary to study all the data in

the universe are ludicrously far beyond the capacity of any imaginable computer. Hawking points out that although we can solve the equations for the movement of two bodies in Newton's theory of gravity, we can't solve them exactly for *three* bodies, not because Newton's theory doesn't work for three bodies but because the math is too complicated. The real universe, needless to say, has more than three bodies in it.

Nor can we predict our health, although we understand the principles that underlie medicine, the principles of chemistry and biology, extremely well. The problem again is that there are too many billions upon billions of details in a real-life system, even when that system is just one human body.

With the Theory of Everything in our hands we'd still be a staggeringly long way from predicting everything. Even if the underlying principles are simple and well understood, the way they work out is enormously complicated. "A minute to learn, the lifetime of the universe to master,"[8] to paraphrase an advertising slogan. "Lifetime of the universe to master" is a gross understatement.

Where does that leave us? What horse will win the Kentucky Derby next year *is* predictable with the Theory of Everything, but no computer can hold all the data or do the math to make the prediction. Is that correct?

There's a further problem. We must look again at the uncertainty principle of quantum mechanics.

The Fuzziness of the Very Small

At the level of the very small, the quantum level of the universe, the uncertainty principle limits our ability to predict things.

Think of all those odd, busy inhabitants of the quantum world, both fermions and bosons. They're an impressive zoo of particles. Among the fermions there are electrons, protons, and neutrons. Each proton or neutron is, in turn, made up of three quarks, which are also fermions. Then we have the bosons: photons (messengers of the electromagnetic force), gravitons (the gravitational force), gluons (the strong force), and W's and Z's (the weak force). It would be helpful to know where all these and many others are, where they're going, and how quickly they're getting there. Can we find out?

You've seen diagrams of atoms like that in Figure 2-1. This is a model proposed by Ernest Rutherford (at the Cavendish Labs in Cambridge) early in our century, which shows electrons orbiting the nucleus of the atom as planets orbit the sun.

We now know that things never really look like this on the quantum level. The orbits of electrons can't be plotted as though electrons were planets. We do better to picture them swarming in a cloud around the nucleus. Why the blur?

It's the uncertainty principle that makes life at the quantum level a fuzzy, imprecise affair, not just for electrons but for all the particles. We'll state it again: Regardless of how we go about trying to observe what happens, we can't find out exactly both the *velocity* (velocity includes both speed and direction) and the *position* of a particle at the same time. The more accurately we measure the velocity, the less accurately we know the position, and vice versa. It's like a seesaw: when the accuracy of one measurement goes up, the accuracy of the other must go down. And nobody can do anything about it. We pin down one measurement only by allowing the other to become more uncertain. We can't scrutinize the quantum world without causing this havoc.

The best we do to describe the activity of a particle is to study all the possible ways it might be moving and then calculate how likely one way is as opposed to another. It becomes a matter of probabilities. We end up saying a particle has *this* probability to be moving—*that* way—or it has *that* probability to be—*here*. Those probabilities are nevertheless very useful information.

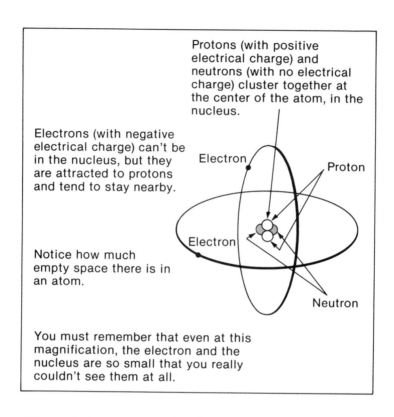

Protons (with positive electrical charge) and neutrons (with no electrical charge) cluster together at the center of the atom, in the nucleus.

Electrons (with negative electrical charge) can't be in the nucleus, but they are attracted to protons and tend to stay nearby.

Electron

Proton

Electron

Notice how much empty space there is in an atom.

Neutron

You must remember that even at this magnification, the electron and the nucleus are so small that you really couldn't see them at all.

Figure 2-1. In the Rutherford model of a helium atom, the electrons orbit the nucleus the way planets orbit the sun. We now know that because of the uncertainty principle of quantum mechanics, electron orbits are not really well-defined paths as shown in this model.

It's a little like predicting the outcome of elections. Election poll experts work with probabilities. When they're dealing with large enough numbers of voters, they come up with statistics that allow them to predict who'll win the election and by what margin, without having to know how each individual will vote. In quantum physics when physicists study a large number of possible paths that particles might follow, the probabilities of their moving thus and so or of being in one place rather than another become concrete information.

Pollsters admit that interviewing an individual can influence a vote by causing the voter to become more aware. Physicists have a similar dilemma. Probing the quantum level influences the answers they find.

Thus far the comparison between predicting elections and studying the quantum level seems a good one. Now it breaks down: On election day, each voter does cast a definite vote one way or another, secret perhaps but not uncertain. If pollsters placed hidden cameras in voting booths—and were not arrested—they could find out how each individual voted. It isn't like that in quantum physics. Physicists have devised ingenious ways of sneaking up on particles, all to no avail. The world of elementary particles does not just *seem* uncertain because we haven't been clever enough to find a successful way to observe it. It *really is* uncertain. It's no wonder Hawking, in his Lucasian lecture, called quantum mechanics "a theory of what we do not know and cannot predict."[9]

Taking this limitation into account, physicists have redefined the goal of science: The Theory of Everything will be a set of laws that make it possible to predict events *up to the limit set by the uncertainty principle,* and that means in many cases we will have to satisfy ourselves with statistical probabilities, not specifics.

Stephen Hawking sums up our problem. In answer to the question whether everything is predetermined either by the Theory of Everything or by God, he says Yes, he thinks it is. "But it might as well not be, because we can never know what is determined. If the theory has determined that we shall die by hanging, then we shall not drown. But you would have to be awfully sure that you were destined for the gallows to put to sea in a

29

small boat during a storm."[10] He regards the idea of free will as "a very good approximate theory of human behavior."[11]

Is There Really a Theory of Everything?

It's only fair to mention that not all physicists believe there is a Theory of Everything, or, if there is, that it's possible for anyone to find it. Some think science will go on refining what we know by making discovery after discovery, opening boxes within boxes, but never arrive at the ultimate box. Others argue that events are not entirely predictable but happen in a random fashion. Some believe God and human beings have far more freedom of give-and-take within this creation than a Theory of Everything would allow. They believe that as in the performance of a great piece of orchestral music, though the notes are written down, there may yet be enormous creativity in the playing of the notes that is not at all predetermined.

Whether a complete theory to explain the universe is within our reach or ever will be, there are those among us who want to make a try. We're intrepid beings with insatiable curiosity. Some of us, like Stephen Hawking, are particularly hard to discourage. Murray Gell-Mann of the California Institute of Technology, another physicist leading the quest, writes:

> *It is the most persistent and greatest adventure in human history, this search to understand the universe, how it works and where it came from. It is difficult to imagine that a handful of residents of a small planet circling an insignificant star in a small galaxy have as their aim a complete understanding of the entire universe, a small speck of creation truly believing it is capable of comprehending the whole.*[12]

3

"You shouldn't believe everything you read."

1942–1965

When Stephen Hawking was twelve, two schoolmates made a bet concerning his future. One bet the other that Stephen "would never come to anything." The stake was a bag of candy.

Young S. W. Hawking was no prodigy. Some reports claim he was brilliant in a haphazard way, but Hawking remembers that he was just another ordinary English schoolboy, slow learning to read, his handwriting the despair of his teachers. He ranked no more than halfway up in his school class, though he now says, in his own defense, "It was a very bright class."[1] Maybe someone might have predicted a career in science or engineering from the fact that Stephen was intensely interested in learning the secrets of how things such as clocks and radios work. He took them apart to find out, but he could seldom put them back together. Stephen was never well coordinated physically, and he wasn't keen on sports or other physical activities. The twelve-year-old who bet against Stephen's success had good reason to think he would win the wager.

31

The other boy probably was just a loyal friend or liked betting on long shots. Maybe he did see things about Stephen that teachers, parents, and Stephen himself couldn't see. Let's hope he's claimed his bag of candy. Because Stephen Hawking, after such an unexceptional beginning, is now one of the intellectual giants of our century—and among its most heroic figures. How such transformations happen is a mystery that biographical details alone cannot explain.

Stephen William Hawking was born during World War II, on January 8, 1942, in Oxford, England. It was a winter of discouragement and fear, not a happy time to be born. Hawking likes to recall that his birth was exactly three hundred years after the death of Galileo, who is called the father of modern science. But few people in January 1942 were thinking about Galileo.

Frank and Isobel Hawking, Stephen's parents, weren't wealthy. Frank was the grandson of a prosperous Yorkshire farmer who, unfortunately for his heirs, went bankrupt in the great agricultural depression of the early twentieth century. Isobel was the second oldest of seven children. Her father was a family doctor in Glasgow, Scotland. When Isobel was twelve, they moved to Devon.

It wasn't easy for either family to scrape together money to send a child to Oxford, but in both cases they did. Frank was at Oxford earlier than Isobel. He became a specialist in tropical medicine. When war broke out, he was in East Africa, and he found his way overland to take ship for England and volunteer for military service. He was assigned instead to medical research.

Isobel held several positions after graduation from Oxford. One was inspector of taxes. She so loathed that job that she gave it up in disgust to became a secretary, a fortunate move, for that was how she met Frank Hawking. They were married in the early years of the war.

In January 1942 the Hawkings were living in Highgate, a northern suburb of London. In the London area hardly a night passed without air raids. However, Germany was not bombing Oxford or Cambridge, the two great English university towns, in return for a British promise not to bomb Heidelberg and Goettingen. Frank and Isobel Hawking decided Isobel should go to Oxford to give birth to their baby in safety. After Stephen's birth they took him back to Highgate. Their home survived the war, although a V-2 rocket hit a few doors away when the Hawkings were absent, causing considerable damage.

After the war the family lived in Highgate until 1950. Dr. Hawking became head of the Division of Parasitology at the National Institute for Medical Research. Then, when Stephen was eight, they moved to St. Alban's, a small cathedral city north of London with a colorful history dating to Roman times.

Stephen had two sisters, Mary and Philippa, and a brother, Edward, who was born when Stephen was thirteen. It was a close family. Their home was full of good books, and Frank and Isobel Hawking believed strongly in the value of education. They planned that at age eleven Stephen would go to Westminster, a famous public school (we would call it a "private" school in America) in the heart of London. Frank Hawking thought his own advancement had been hampered by his parents' poverty and the fact that he hadn't attended a prestigious school. Others with less ability but more social graces were getting ahead of him, or so he felt. Stephen was to have something better.

Unfortunately Stephen was ill at the time of the scholarship examination for Westminster. Instead he attended the local Saint Alban's School, in the shadow of the cathedral, but he believes his education there was at least as good as the one he would have received at Westminster.

By the time Stephen was eight or nine, he was thinking seriously about becoming a scientist. It seemed to him that in science he could find out the truth, not only about clocks and radios but also about everything else around him. Frank Hawking encouraged his son to follow him into medicine, but Stephen found biology too imprecise to suit him. Biologists, he thought, observed and described things but didn't explain them on a fundamental level. Biology also involved detailed drawings, and he wasn't good at drawing. Stephen wanted a subject in which he could look for exact answers and get to the root of things. If he'd known about molecular biology, his career might have been very different.

The educational system in Britain requires that students choose a broad field of interest in their early teens. After that they concentrate in subject areas related to that interest and become more and more specialized. At university, where the course is commonly only three years, they usually study only one subject, as Americans do in graduate school.

At age fourteen Stephen knew that what he wanted to do was "mathematics, more mathematics, and physics." His father called this impractical. There were no jobs in mathematics except teaching. Moreover he wanted Stephen to attend his own college, University College, Oxford, and "Univ" offered no mathematics. Stephen followed his father's advice and studied chemistry, physics, and only a little math, in preparation for entrance to Oxford.

As a teenager Stephen became fascinated with extrasensory perception (ESP). He and his friends tried to control the throw of dice with their minds. However, Stephen's interest turned to disgust when he attended a lecture by someone who had investigated famous ESP studies at Duke University in the United States. The lecturer told his audience that whenever the experiments got results, the experimental techniques were faulty, and whenever the experimental techniques were not faulty, they got no results. Stephen concluded that ESP was a fraud. His skepticism about claims for psychic phenomena hasn't changed. To his way of thinking, people who believe such claims are stalled at the level where he was at age fifteen.

Students who rank no higher than halfway up in their school class seldom get into Oxford unless someone pulls strings behind the scenes. Stephen's lackluster performance in secondary school gave Frank Hawking plenty of cause to think he had better begin pulling strings at Oxford. However, he'd underestimated his son. Stephen made nearly perfect marks on the physics section of the entrance examinations. His interview at Oxford went so brilliantly that there was no question he would be accepted.

In 1959, at age seventeen, Hawking went up to Oxford to study natural science, with an emphasis in physics. By this time he had come to consider mathematics a tool for doing physics and learning how the universe behaves, not as an end in itself.

He entered University College, his father's college and the oldest at Oxford, founded in 1249. "Univ" is in the heart of Oxford, on the High Street, one of many colleges that together make up the university. Oxford's architecture, like Cambridge's, is a magnificent hodgepodge of every style since the Middle Ages. Its intellectual and social traditions predate even its buildings and, like those of any great university, are a mix of authentic intellectual brilliance, pretentious fakery, innocent tomfoolery, and true decadence. For a young man interested in any of these, Hawking's new environment had much to offer.

Nevertheless, for about a year and a half, Hawking was lonely and bored. Many students in his year were considerably older than he because they had taken out time for military service. He wasn't inspired to relieve his boredom by exerting himself academically. He had discovered he could get by better than most by doing virtually no studying at all.

Halfway through his second year Hawking began enjoying Oxford. When Robert Berman, his physics tutor at the time, describes him, it's difficult to believe he's speaking of the same Stephen Hawking who seemed so ordinary a few years earlier and so lonely the previous year."[H]e did, I think, positively make an effort to sort of come down to [the other students'] level and, you know, be one of the boys. If you didn't know about his physics and to some extent his mathematical ability, he wouldn't have told you. . . . He was very popular."[2] Others who remember Hawking in his second and third years at Oxford describe him as lively, buoyant, and adaptable. He wore his hair long, was famous for his wit, and liked classical music and science fiction.

The attitude among most Oxford students in those days, as Hawking describes it, was "very antiwork." "You were supposed either to be brilliant without effort, or to accept your limitations and get a fourth class degree. To work hard to get a better class of degree was regarded as the mark of a gray man, the worst epithet in the Oxford vocabulary." Hawking's freewheeling, independent spirit and casual attitude toward his studies fit right in. In a typical incident one day in class, after reading a solution he had worked out, he wadded up the paper disdainfully and propelled it across the room into the wastepaper basket.

The Oxford physics course was arranged in a way that made it easy to avoid work, or at least easy not to see much urgent need for it. It was a three-year course with no exams until the end of the third year. Hawking calculates he spent on the average about one hour per day studying: about one thousand hours in three years. "I'm not proud of this lack of work," he says. "I'm just describing my attitude at the time, which I shared with most of my fellow students: an attitude of complete boredom and feeling that nothing was worth making an effort for. One result of my illness has been to change all that: When you are faced with the possibility of an early death, it makes you realize that life is worth living, and that there are lots of things you want to do."

Hawking was well accepted by his peers, but Dr. Berman and other dons were beginning to recognize that Hawking had a brilliant mind, "completely different from his contemporaries." "Undergraduate physics was simply not a challenge for him. He did very little work, really, because anything that was do-able he could do. It was only necessary for him to know something could be done, and he could do it without looking to see how other people did it. Whether he had any books I don't know, but he didn't have very many, and he didn't take notes."[3] Another tutor called him the kind of student who liked finding mistakes in the textbooks better than working the problems.

Hawking exerted himself more on the river, rowing and coxing for Univ, than he did at his studies. The cox or coxswain is the person who sits facing the line of rowers and steers the boat with handles attached to the rudder. One sure way to be part of the "in" crowd at Oxford was to be a member of your college rowing team. If intense boredom and a feeling that nothing was worth making an effort for were the prevailing attitudes elsewhere, all that changed on the river. Rowers, coxes, and coaches regularly assembled at the boathouse at dawn, even when there was a crust of ice on the river, to perform arduous calisthenics and lift the racing shell into the water. The merciless practice went on in all weather, up and down the river, coaches bicycling along the towpath exhorting their crews. On race days emotions ran high and crowds of rowdy well-wishers sprinted along the towpath to keep up with their college boats. There were foggy race days when boats appeared and vanished like ghosts, and drenching race days when water filled the bottom of the boat. Boat club dinners in formal dress in the college hall lasted late and ended in battles of wine-soaked linen napkins.

All of it added up to a stupendous feeling of physical well-being, camaraderie, all-stops-out effort, and of living college life to the hilt. Hawking became a popular member of the boating crowd. At the level of intercollege competition he did well. He'd never before been good at a sport, and this was an exhilarating change.

However, at the end of the third year, examinations loomed larger than any boat race. At that point Hawking almost floundered. He'd settled on theoretical physics as his specialty. That meant a choice between two areas for graduate work: cosmology, the study of the very large, or elementary particles, the study of the very small. Hawking chose cosmology. "It just seemed that cosmology was more exciting, because it really did seem to involve the big question: Where did the universe come from?"[4] Fred Hoyle, the most distinguished British astronomer of the time, was at Cambridge. Hawking had applied to do Ph.D. research at Cambridge and been accepted with the condition that he get a "First" from Oxford, the equivalent of graduating with highest honors from an American university.

One thousand hours of study was meager preparation for getting a First. However, an Oxford examination offers a choice from many questions and problems. Hawking was confident he could get through successfully by doing problems in theoretical physics and avoiding any questions that required knowledge of facts. As the examination day approached, his confidence failed. The night before the examination he was too nervous to sleep. The examination went poorly. Hawking ended up disastrously on the borderline between a First and a Second.

Faced with a borderline result, the examiners summoned Hawking for a personal interview. They questioned him about his plans. In spite of the tenseness of the situation, with his future hanging in the balance, Hawking managed to come up with the kind of remark for which he was famous among his friends: "If I get a First, I shall go to Cambridge. If I receive a Second, I will remain at Oxford. So I expect that you will give me a First." He got his First. Dr. Berman said of the examiners: "They were intelligent enough to realize they were talking to someone far cleverer than most of themselves."[5]

Hawking's first year and a half at Oxford had been unhappy. His first years at Cambridge were worse. To his disappointment he didn't get Fred Hoyle for supervisor. Instead he was assigned Denis Sciama, of whom he'd never heard. Hawking's slipshod mathematics background caught up with him, and he found general relativity extremely rough going. These were setbacks, but no more than typical for a first-year graduate student.

Another far more disastrous problem arose. During his third year at Oxford Hawking had been getting clumsy. He'd fallen once or twice for no apparent reason. The following autumn, at Cambridge, he had trouble tying his shoes and sometimes had difficulty talking.

After his first term at Cambridge, when Hawking was home for Christmas break, his father noticed these problems and took him to the family doctor. That doctor referred them to a specialist.

Shortly after his twenty-first birthday in January 1963, Hawking found himself not back at Cambridge for the Lent term but in a hospital for tests. Doctors took a muscle sample from his arm, stuck electrodes into him, and injected radio-opaque fluid into his spine and watched it going up and down with X rays while they tilted the bed on which he lay. After two weeks they released him, telling him vaguely that what he had wasn't a "typical case" and that it wasn't multiple sclerosis. The doctors suggested he go back to Cambridge and get on with his work. "I gathered," Hawking remembers, "that they expected it to continue to get worse, and that there was nothing they could do, except give me vitamins. I could see that they didn't expect them to have much effect. I didn't feel like asking for more details, because they were obviously bad."

Hawking had contracted a rare disease for which there is no known cure, amyotrophic lateral sclerosis, known in America as Lou Gehrig's disease, in Britain as motor neurone disease. It causes a gradual disintegration of the nerve cells in the spinal cord and brain that regulate voluntary muscle activity. The first symptoms are usually weakness and twitching of the hands, and perhaps slurred speech and difficulty in swallowing. As nerve cells disintegrate, the muscles they control atrophy. Eventually this happens to every muscle of the body. Movement becomes impossible. Speech and all other means of communication are lost. Death almost always occurs within two or three years as a result of pneumonia or suffocation when the respiratory muscles fail. The brain remains completely lucid to the end. To some this seems an advantage, to others a horror. Patients in the final stages of the disease are often given morphine, not for pain—there is none—but for panic and depression.

For Stephen Hawking everything had changed. With typical understatement, he describes his reaction: "The realization that I had an incurable disease, that was likely to kill me in a few years, was a bit of a shock. How could something like that happen to me? Why should I be cut off like this? However, while I had been in hospital, I had seen a boy I vaguely knew die of leukemia in the bed opposite me. It had not been a pretty sight. Clearly there were people who were worse off than I. At least, my condition didn't make me feel sick. Whenever I feel inclined to be sorry for myself, I remember that boy."

Nevertheless, at first Hawking went into a deep depression. He didn't know what he ought to do, what was going to happen to him, how quickly he would get worse, or what it would be like. His doctors had told him to continue his Ph.D. research, but that had already been going poorly. This fact was almost as depressing to him as his illness. It seemed pointless to try to continue working toward a doctorate he wouldn't live to receive, nothing but a foolish device for keeping his mind preoccupied while his body was dying. He holed up miserably in his college rooms, but he insists, "Reports in magazine articles that I drank heavily are an exaggeration. I felt somewhat of a tragic character. I took to listening to Wagner.

"My dreams at that time were rather disturbed," he remembers. "Before my condition had been diagnosed, I had been very bored with life. There had not seemed to be anything worth doing. But shortly after I came out of hospital, I dreamt that I was going to be executed. I suddenly realized that there were a lot of worthwhile things I could do, if I were reprieved. Another dream that I had several times was that I would sacrifice my life to save others. After all, if I were going to die anyway, it might as well do some good."

Hawking's doctors hoped his condition would stabilize, but the disease progressed rapidly. They soon informed him that he had only about two years to live. His father appealed to Denis Sciama to help Hawking finish his dissertation early. Sciama, knowing Hawking's potential and unwilling to let him compromise even if he was dying, turned the request down.

Two years passed. The progression of the disease slowed. "I didn't die. In fact, although there was a cloud hanging over my future, I found to my surprise that I was enjoying life in the present more than before." He had to use a cane, but his condition wasn't all that bad. Total disability and death, though still a not-too-distant certainty, were postponed. Sciama suggested that since he was going to live a while longer, he ought to finish his thesis. Hawking had his reprieve, a precarious and temporary one, but life *was* precious and full of worthwhile things.

At a New Year's party in St. Alban's, where he was visiting his family in January 1963, just before he entered the hospital for tests, Hawking had met Jane Wilde. She'd also grown up in St. Alban's, but they hadn't met before. Jane was younger than he, just finishing up at Saint Alban's High School and planning to enter Westfield College in London the next autumn as a language student. To her this disheveled graduate student seemed terribly intelligent, eccentric, and rather arrogant. But he was interesting, and she liked his wit. He told her he was studying cosmology. She didn't know what that meant.

When Jane met him again after his release from the hospital, "he was really in quite a pathetic state. I think he'd lost the will to live. He was very confused."[6] She wasn't, however, put off by his physical or mental condition. She was a rather shy teenager, but serious-minded, with a faith in God ingrained from childhood by her mother and a belief that good can come out of any disaster. Hawking thought she was "a very nice girl."[7] He admired her energy and her optimism and gradually found them contagious. The friendship developed slowly, but after a while the two began to realize, in Jane's word, "that together we could make something worthwhile of our lives."[8]

After a courtship divided between London and Cambridge, Stephen Hawking and Jane Wilde became engaged. As she tells it: "I wanted to find some purpose to my existence, and I suppose I found it in the idea of looking after him. But we were in love, we got married, there didn't seem much choice in the matter. I just decided what I was going to do, and I did it."[9]

For Stephen that made "all the difference." "The engagement changed my life. It gave me something to live for. It made me determined to live. Without the help that Jane has given I would not have been able to carry on, nor have had the will to do so."

With his love for Jane Wilde, Hawking's natural buoyancy returned. He made progress with his studies. He decided to count himself supremely lucky that his illness would never touch his mind, no matter how it might paralyze his body. Work in theoretical physics was going to take place almost entirely in his mind. It was one of the few careers he might have chosen in which physical disability wouldn't be a serious handicap.

To us this attitude sounds courageous, but it embarrasses Hawking to hear himself described that way. It would have been courageous and require tremendous willpower, he thinks, to have chosen such a difficult course deliberately, but that wasn't how it happened. He simply did the only thing possible. As he puts it, "One has to be grown up enough to realize that life is not fair. You just have to do the best you can in the situation you are in."[10]

Perhaps this is as good a moment as any to digress a little and point out that as far as Hawking is concerned, the less made of his physical problems the better. If this book were to talk about his scientific work and fail entirely to mention that doing such work possibly represents more of an achievement for him than it would for most people, that would suit him fine. One of the most important things you can learn about Stephen Hawking is how unimportant his disability is. It isn't

43

accurate to call him a sick man. Health involves much more than physical condition, and in this broader sense, for most of his life he's been one of the healthiest persons around. That's the message that comes through loud and clear in his writing and in most of the things written about him, and it is even more apparent when you're with him. That's the Hawking image, and though we should take seriously his warning "You shouldn't believe everything you read," it isn't a fake image.

Meanwhile the most immediate problem for Stephen Hawking was that no marriage was possible until he had a job, and no job was possible until he had a Ph.D. He began looking for an idea with which to complete his thesis.

Hawking had read about a theory of the British mathematician and physicist Roger Penrose concerning what happens when a star has no nuclear fuel left to burn and collapses under the force of its own gravity. Penrose, building on earlier work by such physicists as Subrahmanyan Chandrasekhar and John A. Wheeler, claimed that even if the collapse isn't perfectly smooth and symmetrical, the star will nevertheless be crushed to a tiny point of infinite density and infinite curvature of spacetime, a **singularity** at the heart of a **black hole.**

Hawking took off from there by reversing the direction of time, imagining a point of infinite density and infinite curvature of spacetime—a singularity—exploding outward and expanding. Suppose, he suggested, the universe began like that. Suppose spacetime, curled up tight in a tiny, dimensionless point, exploded in what we call the Big Bang and expanded until it looks the way it does today. Might it have happened like that? *Must* it have happened like that?

With these questions, Hawking began the intellectual adventure that has continued for more than twenty-five years. As he says, "I started working hard for the

44

first time in my life. To my surprise, I found I liked it. Maybe it is not really fair to call it work."

The job Hawking applied for was a research fellowship at one of the colleges that make up Cambridge University, Gonville and Caius, or Caius (pronounced "keys") for short. He remembers that Jane came up from London for a visit at that time. "I was hoping that Jane would type my application, but she had her arm in plaster, having broken it. I must admit that I was less sympathetic than I should have been. However, it was her left arm, so she was able to write out my application to my dictation, and I got someone else to type it."

Jane's arm was not the worst setback he encountered applying for the Caius fellowship. He was asked to name two persons as references. His supervisor, Denis Sciama, suggested Herman Bondi, an expert on general relativity at Kings College, London. "I had met him a couple of times, and he had communicated a paper I had written to the Royal Society. I asked him [about giving a reference] after a lecture he gave in Cambridge. He looked at me in a vague way, and said, yes, he would. Obviously, he didn't remember me, for, when the College wrote to him for a reference, he replied that he had not heard of me." That should have shattered Hawking's chances. It would today, with so many applying for research fellowships, but he was fortunate. "Those were quieter times. The College wrote to tell me of the embarrassing reply of my referee. My supervisor got on to Bondi, and refreshed his memory. Bondi then wrote me a reference that was probably far better than I deserved. Anyway I got the fellowship."

In 1965 at age twenty-three Hawking received his fellowship at Caius. In July of that year he and Jane were married.

Theoretical physics is full of paradoxes. It seems fitting that one of our greatest theoretical physicists is a

man whose enthusiasm for life was awakened by a tragedy that ought to have embittered and destroyed him,
and that his meteoric rise as a scientist began with the
practical need for a thesis topic so that he could get a
job and get married. With what simplicity Hawking describes it: In spite of the Wagner, the tragic hero self-
image, and the dreams; a year, maybe more, of
depression, but then "I was happier than I'd been before."

4

"The big question was, Was there a beginning or not?"

1965–1970

After their wedding in July 1965 and a short honeymoon near Cambridge in Suffolk, which was all they could afford, Stephen and Jane Hawking flew to America for a general relativity summer school at Cornell University in upper New York State. For Hawking this was an opportunity to meet top people in his field. However, he remembers the experience as "a mistake." "It put quite a strain on our marriage, specially as we stayed in a dormitory that was full of couples with noisy small children."[1]

Back in Cambridge in the autumn, Jane Hawking had another year to go to complete her undergraduate degree at London University. The plan was that Hawking would fend for himself during the week while she lived in London. She would join him for the weekends. Since he couldn't walk far or cycle, he needed lodgings near his department.

Before going to America they had applied for a flat being built in Cambridge market square, but that wasn't ready for occupancy. The bursar at Caius College, where

Hawking was now a Research Fellow, had earlier declared that Caius policy was *not* to help Fellows find housing. Relenting only slightly, he now offered the Hawkings one room in a graduate student hostel and charged them double because there would be two of them living there on weekends.

Hawking's problems have a way of turning into advantages. Maybe Jane Hawking's philosophy is correct. Three days after moving into the hostel, they discovered a small house available for three months. It was ideally located in a picturesque row facing the garden of a historic Cambridge church, Little Saint Mary's, only a hundred yards from the Department of Applied Mathematics and Theoretical Physics. Stephen Hawking was able to walk that distance, and he acquired a small three-wheeled car to drive when he needed to get to the Institute of Astronomy in the countryside near town. Before the three months' lease ended, they found that another house in the lane was unoccupied. A kindly neighbor located the owner in Dorset and scolded her for having her house vacant while a young couple had no place to live. The owner agreed to rent. A few years later the Hawkings bought that house, and Stephen Hawking's parents gave them money to fix it up.

During the year after she and Hawking were married, Jane Hawking's talent for organization became obvious. She managed the weekly commute, finished her degree at London University, and typed her husband's Ph.D. dissertation for him. All of that behind her, the Hawkings decided to start a family. Their first son, Robert, was born in 1967. It was four years since doctors had told Stephen Hawking he had two years to live. He was still on his feet, and he was a father. Jane Hawking recalls, "It obviously gave Stephen a great new impetus, being responsible for this tiny creature."[2]

People who remember Hawking in the Department of Applied Maths and Theoretical Physics (DAMTP) in the late 1960s recall his making his way around the corridors with a cane, supporting himself against the wall. He spoke with what sounded like a slight speech impediment. More than that, they remember his brashness in sessions involving some of the world's most distinguished scientists. While other young researchers kept a reverent silence, Hawking daringly asked unexpected and penetrating questions and clearly knew what he was talking about. His reputation as "a genius," "another Einstein," began then. In spite of Hawking's ready wit and popularity, that reputation and his physical problems distanced him from some in the department. One acquaintance told me, "He was very friendly always, but at the same time, some felt a little shy about asking him out with the gang for a beer at the pub." It's no wonder Hawking feels it's been a problem preventing people from thinking of him as "anything less or more than simply human."[3]

In the late 1960s, Hawking's physical condition began deteriorating again. He had to use crutches. Then it became difficult for him to get about even with crutches. Hawking waged a pitched battle against the loss of his independence. A visitor remembers watching him spend fifteen minutes getting up the stairs to bed on his crutches, determined to do it without help.

This determination sometimes seemed to be pigheadedness. Hawking refused to make concessions to his illness, even when those "concessions" were practical steps to make things easier for him and make him less a burden to others. It was his battle. He would fight it his way. His way was to regard any concession as caving in, an admission of defeat, and to resist as long as possible. "Some people would call it determination, some obstinacy," says Jane Hawking. "I've called it both at one time or another. I suppose that's what's kept him going."[4] John Boslough, who wrote a book about Hawking in the early 1980s, called him "the toughest man I have ever met."[5] Even with a bad cold or flu, Hawking rarely missed a day of work.

While Hawking refused to make concessions to his illness, Jane Hawking learned to make no concessions to him. This was *her* way of fighting and part of her campaign to keep his life as normal as possible.

Boslough also described Hawking as a "gentle, witty man," who quickly made you forget about his physical problems. That "gentle" wit cut through all nonsense and pretension. Hawking's ability to make light of himself, his problems, and even the science he was so keen on was awe-inspiring. It made him tremendously popular and most of the time eclipsed the feelings of "differentness." For many he became, of all those in the department, the most fun to be around.

Hawking seems to have been following, without probably ever having read it, the advice Louisa May Alcott's mother gave her family in times of overwhelming distress: "Hope and keep busy." At least as far as anyone could tell, his science occupied his mind far more than concern about canes and crutches and stairs. His almost obsessive enjoyment of his work set the tone of his life. In the late 1960s he was finding out what the universe is like and how it might have begun—what he describes as playing "the game of universe." In order to understand the work he was immersed in, we have to go back thirty-five years.

The Universe Is Expanding

Today we take it for granted that we live in a lacy spiral disk galaxy and that there are many other galaxies more or less like it in the universe, with vast stretches of space between. Early in our century not everyone accepted this picture. It was the American astronomer Edwin Hubble who, in the 1920s, showed that there are indeed many galaxies besides our own. Is there any pattern to the movement of these galaxies? It was Hubble again who showed that there is, with one of the most revolutionary discoveries of our century: The distant galaxies are all moving away from us. The universe is expanding.

Hubble found that the more distant a galaxy is, the more rapidly it's moving away from us: twice as far, twice as fast. Some extremely distant galaxies are receding as fast as two-thirds the speed of light. Does that mean every star in the universe is moving away from us? No. Our near neighbors are milling around, some approaching, some receding. It's between clusters of galaxies that space is expanding. The most helpful way to think of the expansion of the universe is not as things rushing away from one another but as space between them swelling. Imagine a loaf of raisin bread rising in the oven. As the dough swells, the raisins move apart. "Twice as far, twice as fast" works with raisins as well as with galaxies.

If galaxies are receding from us and from each other, then unless something has changed drastically somewhere along the line, they used to be much closer together. In fact, at some moment in the past, wouldn't they all have been in exactly the same place? All the enormous amount of matter in the universe packed in a single point, infinitely dense?

That isn't the only possible history of an expanding universe. Perhaps there was once a universe something like ours, and that universe contracted, with all its galaxies getting closer together, looking as though they were on collision course. But the galaxies and the stars in them, and the atoms and particles, of course, had other motion in addition to the motion that was drawing them straight toward one another. The planets were orbiting stars, for instance. The result might have been that, instead of meeting in a point of infinite density, the galaxies, or the particles that made them up, missed one another, flew past, and the universe expanded again until it looks the way it does today. Could it have happened like that? Which way did it happen? These were questions Hawking began to consider in his Ph.D. thesis. "The big question was," says Hawking, "was there a beginning or not?"[6]

His search for an answer began, as we mentioned in Chapter 3, with an idea introduced by Roger Penrose in 1965. Penrose's idea concerned the way some stars may end up—something that three years later was going to be given the spectacular name *black hole* by John Archibald Wheeler at Princeton. The concept combined what we know about gravity with what general relativity tells us about the behavior of light.

What Do We Know about Gravity and Light?

Gravity is the most familiar of the four forces. We all learned early in life that it's gravity you blame when your ice cream cone splats on the rug or when you fall off a swing. If you were asked to guess whether gravity is a very weak or a very strong force, you might answer "incredibly strong." You would be wrong. It's by far the weakest of the four forces. The gravity that's so conspicuous in our everyday lives is the gravity of this great hulk of a planet we live on, the combined gravity of every particle in it. The contribution of each individual particle is infinitesimal. It takes sensitive instruments to detect the faint gravitational attraction between small, everyday objects. However, because gravity always attracts, never repels, it has a talent for adding up.

The physicist John Wheeler likes to think of gravity as a sort of universal democratic system. Every particle has a vote that can affect every other particle in the universe. When particles band together and vote as a bloc (in a star, for instance, or in our earth), then they wield more influence. The very weak gravitational attraction of the individual particles in large bodies like the earth adds up to a significant force: an influential voting bloc.

The more matter-particles there are making up a body, the more mass that body has. Mass is not the same as size. Mass is a measure of how much matter is in an object, how many votes are in the voting bloc (regardless of how densely or loosely the matter is packed), and how much the object resists any attempt to change its speed or direction.

Sir Isaac Newton, Lucasian Professor of Mathematics at Cambridge in the 1600s, the same position Hawking holds today, discovered laws explaining how gravity works in more-or-less normal circumstances. First, bodies are not "at rest" in the universe. They don't just sit still until some force comes along to push or pull them and then later "run down" and sit still again. Instead, a body left completely undisturbed continues to move in a straight line without changing speed. It's best to think of everything in the universe as being in motion. We can measure our speed or direction in relation to other objects in the universe, but we can't measure them in relation to absolute stillness or anything that resembles absolute north, south, east, west, or up or down.

For example, if our moon were alone in space, it would not sit still but rather move in a straight line without changing its speed. (Of course, if it were truly all alone, there would be no way to tell it was doing this, nothing to which we could relate its motion.) But the moon isn't all alone. A force known as gravity acts on the moon to change its speed and direction. Where does that force come from? It comes from a nearby voting bloc of particles (a massive object) known as the earth. The moon resists the change. It tries to keep moving in a straight line. How well it's able to resist depends on how many votes are in *it*, how massive it is. Meanwhile, the moon's gravity also affects the earth. The most obvious result is the ocean tides.

Newton's theory tells us that the amount of mass a body has affects how strong the pull of gravity is between it and another body. Other factors remaining equal, the greater the mass, the greater the attraction. If the earth were double its present mass, the attraction of gravity between the earth and the moon would be double what it currently is. Any change in the mass of either the earth or the moon would change the strength of the gravitational pull between them. Newton also discovered that the farther apart bodies are, the weaker the pull between them is. If the moon were twice its present distance from the earth, the pull of gravity between the earth and the moon would be only one-fourth as strong (see **Newton's theory of gravity** in the Glossary).

Newton's theory of gravity is an extremely successful theory. It wasn't improved on for over two hundred years. We still use it, though we now know that it fails in some circumstances, such as when gravitational forces become enormously strong (near a black hole, for instance) or when bodies are moving at near light speed.

Albert Einstein, early in our own century, saw a problem with Newton's theory. Newton, you remember, told us that the strength of gravity between two objects is related to the distance between them. If this is true, then if someone took the sun and moved it farther from the earth, the force of gravity between the earth and the sun would change instantly. Is this possible?

Einstein's theory of special relativity recognized that the speed of light measures the same no matter where you are in the universe or how you're moving and that nothing can move faster than the speed of light. Light from the sun takes about eight minutes to reach earth. We always see the sun as it was eight minutes ago. So, move the sun farther from the earth; the earth won't find out this has happened and feel any effect of the change for eight minutes. For eight minutes we'll continue to orbit just as though the sun hadn't moved.

In other words, the effect of the gravity of one body on the other cannot change instantaneously because gravity can't move faster than the speed of light. Information about how far away the sun is cannot move instantaneously across space. It can move no faster than about 186,000 miles (300,000 kilometers) per second.

It's obvious that when we talk about things moving in the universe, it's not realistic to talk in terms of only the three dimensions of space. If no information can travel faster than the speed of light, things out there at astronomical distances simply don't exist for us or for each other without a time factor. Describing the universe in three dimensions is as inadequate as describing a cube in two. It makes much more sense to include the time dimension, admit there are really four dimensions, and talk of spacetime.

Einstein spent several years attempting to find a theory of gravity that would work with what he'd discovered about light and motion at near light speed. In 1915 he introduced the theory of general relativity. He asked us to think of gravity not as a force acting between bodies but in terms of the shape, the curvature, of four-dimensional spacetime itself. In general relativity gravity is the geometry of the universe.

Bryce DeWitt, of the University of Texas, suggests we begin thinking about this curvature by imagining someone who believes the earth is flat trying to draw a grid on the earth.

The result can be seen from an airplane on any clear day over the cultivated regions of the Great Plains. The land is subdivided by east-west and north-south roads into square-mile sections. The east-west roads often extend in unbroken lines for many miles, but not the north-south roads. Following a road northward, there are abrupt jogs to the east or west every few miles.

The jogs are forced by the curvature of the earth. If the jogs were eliminated, the roads would crowd together, creating sections of less than a square mile. In the three-dimensional case one can imagine building a giant scaffold in space out of straight rods of equal length joined at angles of precisely 90 degrees and 180 degrees. If space is flat, the construction of the scaffold would proceed without difficulty. If space is curved, one would eventually have to begin shortening the rods or stretching them to make them fit."[7]

According to Einstein the curvature is caused by the presence of mass or energy. Every massive body contributes to the curvature of spacetime. Things going "straight ahead" in the universe are forced to follow curved paths. Imagine a trampoline (Figure 4-1). In its center lies a bowling ball, which causes a depression in the rubber sheet. Try to roll a golf ball in a straight line past the bowling ball. The golf ball will certainly change direction slightly when it meets the depression caused by the bowling ball. It will probably do more than that: It may describe an ellipse and roll back in your direction. Something like that happens as the moon tries to continue in a straight line past the earth. The earth warps spacetime as the bowling ball warps the rubber sheet. The moon's orbit is the nearest thing to a straight line in warped spacetime.

You'll notice that Einstein was describing the same phenomenon that Newton described. To Einstein a massive object warps spacetime. To Newton a massive object sends out a force. The result, in each case, is a change in the direction of a second object. According to the theory of general relativity, "gravitational field" and "curvature" are the same thing.

If you calculate planetary orbits in our solar system

56

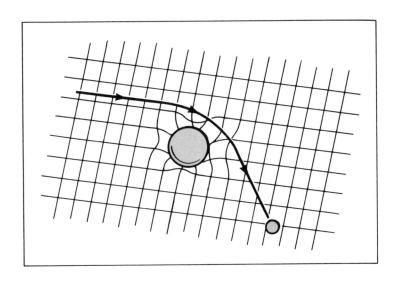

Figure 4-1. A bowling ball bends a rubber sheet where it lies. If you try to roll a smaller ball past the bowling ball, the path of the smaller ball will be bent when it encounters the depression caused by the bowling ball. In a similar manner, mass bends spacetime. Paths of objects in spacetime are bent when they encounter the curvature caused by a more massive object.

using Newton's theories and then calculate them again using Einstein's, you get almost precisely the same orbits, except in the case of Mercury. Because Mercury is the nearest planet to the sun, it's affected more than the others by the sun's gravity. Einstein's theory predicts a result of this nearness which is slightly different from the result predicted by Newton's theory. Observation shows that Mercury's orbit fits Einstein's prediction better than Newton's.

Einstein's theory predicts that other things besides moons and planets are affected by the warp of spacetime. Photons (particles of light) have to travel a warped path. If a beam of light is traveling from a distant star and its path takes it close to our sun, the warping of spacetime near the sun causes the path to bend inward toward the sun a bit, just as the path of the golf ball bends inward toward the bowling ball in our model. Perhaps the path of light bends in such a way that the light finally hits the earth. Our sun is too bright for us to see such starlight except during an eclipse of the sun. If we see it then and don't realize the sun is bending the path of the star's light, we're going to get the wrong idea about which direction the beam of light is coming from and where that star actually is in the sky (Figure 4-2). Astronomers make use of this effect. They measure the mass of objects in space by measuring how much they bend the paths of light from distant stars. The greater the mass of the "bender," the greater the bending.

We've been talking about gravity in terms of what we observe on the large scale. That, of course, is the scale on which gravity becomes conspicuous—in stars, galaxies, even the entire universe—and that is the scale Hawking was dealing with in the late sixties. However, you'll remember from Chapter 2 that gravity can also be looked at in terms of the very small, the quantum level. In fact, unless we can study it there, we will never get it unified with the other three forces, two of which work exclusively on that level. The quantum-mechanical way of looking at the gravitational attraction between the earth and the moon is to picture it as an exchange of gravitons (the bosons, or messenger particles, of the gravitational force) between the particles that make up those two bodies.

With that background, we'll treat ourselves to a little science fiction.

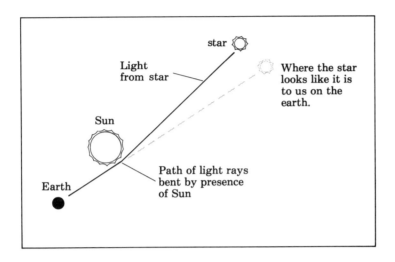

Figure 4-2. Because mass causes curvature of spacetime, the path of light traveling from a distant star bends as it passes a massive body like the sun. Notice the difference between the position of the star as we see it from the earth and its true position.

The Day the Earth Got Squeezed

Remind yourself what the force of gravity feels like on earth (Figure 4-3a). Pretend you take a vacation in space. During your absence something odd happens to the earth: it gets squeezed. After that it's only half its original size. It still has the same mass, pressed together more tightly. Returning from your vacation, your spacecraft hovers for a while at the place in space where the earth's surface used to be before the squeezing. You feel

(a)

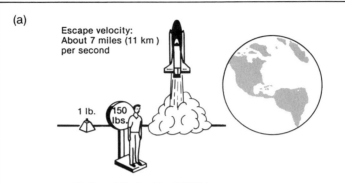

Escape velocity:
About 7 miles (11 km)
per second

1 lb. 150 lbs.

Radius of Earth: About 6500 km

(b)

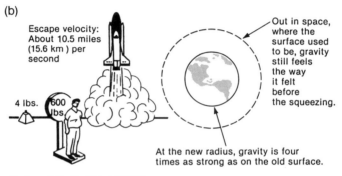

Escape velocity:
About 10.5 miles
(15.6 km) per
second

Out in space,
where the
surface used
to be, gravity
still feels
the way
it felt
before
the squeezing.

4 lbs. 600 lbs.

At the new radius, gravity is four
times as strong as on the old surface.

Radius of Earth: About 3,250 km

(c)

Out in space, where the surface used to be
before there was any squeezing, gravity
still feels as it did before the squeezing.

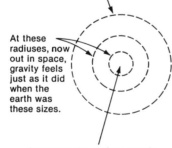

At these
radiuses, now
out in space,
gravity feels
just as it did
when the
earth was
these sizes.

The whole earth is now about the
size of a pea.

Escape velocity: More than
186,000 miles (300,000 km.)
per second, the speed of light.

The weights of the person and the
block no longer have any meaning,
they've been torn apart.

Gravity on the surface now is
so strong that not even light can escape.

as heavy there as you did before you went away. The pull of the earth's gravity there hasn't changed, because neither your mass nor that of the earth has changed, and you are still the same distance as before from the earth's center of gravity. (Remember Newton!) The moon, out beyond you, still orbits as before. However, when you land on the new surface (a much smaller radius, quite a bit nearer the earth's center of gravity), the gravity on that new surface is four times what you remember on the earth's surface before the squeezing. You feel much heavier (Figure 4-3b).

What if something far more dramatic happened? What if the earth were squeezed to the size of a pea—all the mass of the earth, billions of tons, squeezed into that tiny space? Gravity on its surface would be so strong that escape velocity would be greater than the speed of light. Even light couldn't escape. The earth would be a black hole. However, at the radius out in space where the surface of the earth was before any squeezing, the pull of the earth's gravity would still feel just the same as it does to us today (Figure 4-3c). The moon would still be orbiting just as before.

As far as we know, that story can't happen. Planets don't become black holes. However, there's a good chance some stars do. Let's retell the story, this time with a star.

Begin with a star that has a mass about ten times that of the sun. The star's radius is about 3 million kilometers, about five times that of the sun. Escape velocity is about 1,000 kilometers per second. Such a star has

Figure 4-3. The day the earth gets squeezed

a life span of about a hundred million years, during which a life-and-death tug-of-war goes on within it.

On one side of the tug-of-war is gravity: the attraction of every particle in the star for every other. It was gravity that pulled particles in a gas together to form the star in the first place. The pull is even more powerful now that the particles are closer together. The gravity team in the tug-of-war tries to make the star collapse.

On the opposing side of the tug-of-war is the pressure of the gas in the star. This pressure comes from heat released when hydrogen nuclei in the star collide and merge to form helium nuclei. The heat makes the star shine and creates enough pressure to resist gravity and prevent the star from collapsing.

For a hundred million years the tug-of-war continues. Then the star runs out of fuel: no more hydrogen to convert into helium. Some stars then convert helium into heavier elements, but that gives them only a short reprieve. When there's no more pressure to counteract gravity, the star shrinks. As it does, the gravity on its surface becomes stronger and stronger, in the same way that gravity on the earth's surface did in the shrinking earth story. It won't have to shrink to the size of a pea to become a black hole. When the 10-solar-mass star's radius is about 20 miles (30 kilometers), escape velocity on its surface will have increased to 186,000 miles (300,000 kilometers) per second, the speed of light. When light can no longer escape, the star becomes a black hole (Figure 4-4). (For reasons we won't discuss in this book, stars less massive than about 8 solar masses probably don't shrink all the way to become black holes. Only more massive stars become black holes.)

After the escape velocity on its surface is greater than the speed of light, we don't have to ask whether the star goes on shrinking. Even if it doesn't, we still have a black hole. Remember how gravity at the original radius never changed in the earth-shrinking story. Whether our star goes on shrinking to a point of infinite

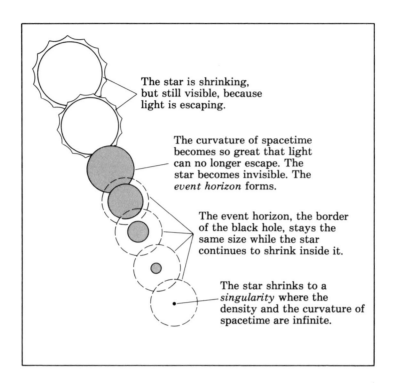

The star is shrinking, but still visible, because light is escaping.

The curvature of spacetime becomes so great that light can no longer escape. The star becomes invisible. The *event horizon* forms.

The event horizon, the border of the black hole, stays the same size while the star continues to shrink inside it.

The star shrinks to a *singularity* where the density and the curvature of spacetime are infinite.

Figure 4-4. A star collapses and becomes a black hole.

density or stops shrinking just within the radius where escape velocity reaches the speed of light, gravity at that radius is going to feel the same, as long as the star's mass doesn't change. Escape velocity at that radius is the speed of light and will stay the speed of light. Light coming from the star will find escape impossible. Nearby beams of light from distant stars won't only be bent; they may curl around the black hole several times before escaping or falling in (Figure 4-5). If the light enters the black hole, it will never escape. Nothing can achieve a greater velocity than the speed of light. What a profound "blackout" we have! No light, no reflection, no radiation of any kind (radio, microwave, X ray, and so on), no sound, no sight, no space probe, absolutely no information can escape. A black hole indeed!

The radius where escape velocity is the speed of light becomes the border of the black hole, the radius-of-no-return: the **event horizon.** Hawking and Penrose, in the late 1960s, suggested defining a black hole as an area of the universe, or a "set of events," from which it's impossible for anything to escape to a distance. That's now the accepted definition. A black hole, with its event horizon for an outer boundary, is shaped like a sphere, or, if it's rotating, a bulged-out sphere that looks elliptical when seen from the side (or would, if you could see it). The event horizon is marked by the paths in space-time of rays of light that hover just on the edge of that spherical area, not being pulled in but unable to escape. Gravity at that radius is strong enough to stop their escape but not strong enough to pull them back in. Will you see them as a great orb shimmering in space? No. If the photons can't escape from that radius, they can't reach your eyes. In order for you to see something, photons from it have to reach your eyes.

It's the mass of the black hole that determines its size. If you want to figure the radius of a black hole (the radius at which the event horizon forms), take the solar mass of the black hole (the same as for the star that collapsed to form it—unless that star lost mass earlier in the collapse) and multiply by 2 for miles or 3 for kilometers. You'll find that a 10-solar-mass black hole has its event horizon at a radius of 20 miles (30 kilometers). It's clear that if the mass changes, the radius where the event horizon is also changes. The black hole changes in size. We'll talk more about this possibility later.

Having drawn the curtain at the event horizon, the star has complete privacy, while any light it emits (any picture of itself that otherwise would be viewed from elsewhere in the universe) is pulled back in. Penrose

64

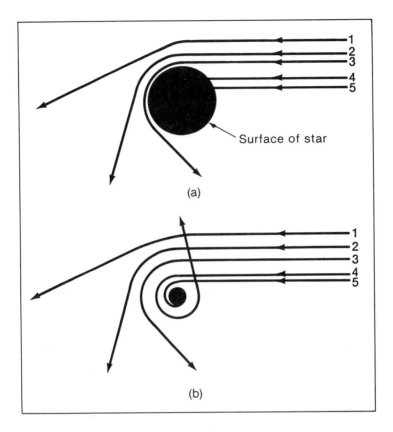

Figure 4-5. In (a), particles from space move toward a star. The paths of particles 1, 2, and 3 are bent as they pass the star. The closer to the star, the greater the bending. Particles 4 and 5 hit the surface of the star. In (b), we see the same particles moving toward the star after it has become a black hole. The paths of particles 1, 2, and 3 are bent exactly as before, because the spacetime outside a star is the same as the spacetime outside a black hole of the same mass. (Recall the shrinking earth.) Particle 4 circles the black hole and then escapes. It might circle it many times. Particle 5 is captured by the black hole.

wanted to know whether the star would go on collapsing—or just what would happen to it. He discovered that a star collapsing as we've described has all its matter trapped inside its own surface by the force of its own gravity. Even if the collapse isn't perfectly spherical and smooth, the star does go on collapsing. The surface eventually shrinks to zero size, with all the matter still trapped inside. Our enormous 10-solar-mass star is then confined not just in a region with a 20-mile (30-kilometer) radius (where its event horizon is), but rather in a region of *zero* radius—zero volume. Mathematicians call that a **singularity.** At such a singularity the density of matter is infinite. Spacetime curvature is infinite, and beams of light aren't just curled around: they're wound up infinitely tightly.

General relativity predicts the existence of singularities, but in the early 1960s few took this prediction seriously. Physicists thought that a star of great enough mass undergoing gravitational collapse *might* form a singularity. Penrose showed that if the universe obeys general relativity, it *must*.

"There Is a Singularity in Our Past"

Penrose's idea set fire to Hawking. Hawking realized that if he reversed the direction of time so that the collapse became an expansion, everything in Penrose's theory would still hold. If general relativity tells us that any star which collapses beyond a certain point must *end* in a singularity, then it also tells us that any expanding universe must have *begun* as a singularity. Hawking found that for this to be true the universe must be like what scientists call a Friedmann model. What is a Friedmann model of the universe?

Until Hubble demonstrated that the universe is expanding, belief in a static universe (one that isn't changing in size) was very strong. When Einstein produced the theory of general relativity in 1915, that theory predicted the universe was expanding. However, Einstein was so sure it wasn't that he revised his theory. He put in a "cosmological constant" to balance gravity. Without this cosmological constant the theory of general relativity predicted what we now know to be true: the universe is changing in size.

A Russian physicist, Alexander Friedmann, decided to take Einstein's theory at face value without the cosmological constant. Doing so, he predicted what Hubble would prove in 1929: The universe is expanding.

Friedmann started with two assumptions: (1) the universe looks much the same in whatever direction you look (except for nearby things like the shape of our Milky Way galaxy and our solar system); (2) the universe looks like this from wherever you are in the universe. In other words, no matter where you travel in space, the universe *still* looks much the same in whatever direction you look.

Friedmann's first assumption is fairly easy to accept. The second isn't. We don't have any scientific evidence for or against it. Hawking says, "We believe it only on grounds of modesty: it would be most remarkable if the universe looked the same in every direction around us, but not around other points in the universe!"[8] Perhaps remarkable, but not impossible, you may argue. Modesty seems no more logical a reason for believing something than pride. However, physicists tend to agree with Friedmann.

In Friedmann's model of the universe all the galaxies move away from one another. The farther apart two galaxies are, the more rapidly they move away from one another. This agrees with what Hubble observed. According to Friedmann, wherever you travel in space you'll still find all the galaxies moving away from you. In order to understand this, imagine an ant crawling on a balloon that has evenly spaced dots painted on it. You have to pretend the ant can't see the dimension that would allow it to look "out" from the surface. Nor is it aware that the balloon has an interior. The ant's universe involves only the surface of the balloon. It looks the same in any direction. No matter where the ant crawls on the balloon, it sees as many dots ahead of it as behind. If the balloon is getting larger, the ant sees all the dots move away, no matter where it stands on the surface. The balloon "universe" fits Friedmann's two assumptions: It looks the same in all directions. It looks the same no matter where you are in it.

What else can we say about the balloon universe? It isn't infinite in size. The surface has dimensions we can measure, like the surface of the earth. No one would suggest that the surface of the earth is infinite in size. However, it also has no boundaries, no ends. Regardless of where the ant crawls on the surface, it never comes up against any barrier, finds any end to the surface, or falls off an edge. It eventually gets back to where it started.

In Friedmann's original model space is like that, with three dimensions rather than two. Gravity bends space around onto itself. The universe is not infinite in size, but neither does it have any end, any boundary. A spaceship will never get to a place in space where the universe ends. That may be difficult to understand, because we tend to think of *infinite* as meaning "having no end." The two do not have the same meaning.

Hawking points out that although the idea of circumnavigating the universe and ending up where you started makes great science fiction, it doesn't work, at least with this Friedmann model. You'd have to break the speed limit of the universe (the speed of light)—which isn't allowed—to get all the way around before the universe ends. It's an extremely large balloon. We're extremely small ants.

Time in this Friedmann model, like space, isn't infinite. It can be measured. Time, *unlike* space, *does* have boundaries: a beginning and an end. Look at Figure 4-6a. The distance between two galaxies at the beginning of time is zero. They move apart. The expansion is slow enough and there is enough mass in the universe so that eventually gravitational attraction stops the expansion and causes the universe to contract. The galaxies move toward each other again. At the end of time the distance between them is once again zero. That may be what our universe is like.

Figure 4-6b & c shows two other possible models that would also obey Friedmann's assumptions (that the universe looks the same in every direction and that it looks the same from wherever you are in the universe). In Figure 4-6b, the expansion is much more rapid. Gravity can't stop it, though it does slow it a little. In Figure 4-6c, the universe is expanding just fast enough not to collapse, but not as fast as in Figure 4-6b. The speed at which galaxies are moving apart grows smaller and smaller, but they always continue to move apart. If the universe is like either of these two models, space is infinite. It doesn't curve back around onto itself.

Which model fits our universe? Will the universe collapse someday or go on expanding forever? We don't at present have enough evidence to answer that. It depends on how much mass there is in the universe: how many votes there are in the entire democracy. It will take much more mass than we *presently* observe to close the universe.

Penrose's theory about stars' collapsing and becoming singularities only worked with a universe infinite in space that will go on expanding forever (as in Figures 4-6b and 4-6c), not collapse (as in Figure 4-6a). Hawking first set out to prove that a universe infinite in space not only would have singularities in black holes but also must have begun as a singularity. He was confident enough by the time he finished his thesis to write, "There is a singularity in our past."[9]

However, what if Friedmann's *first* model was correct, where the universe is not infinite in space and even-

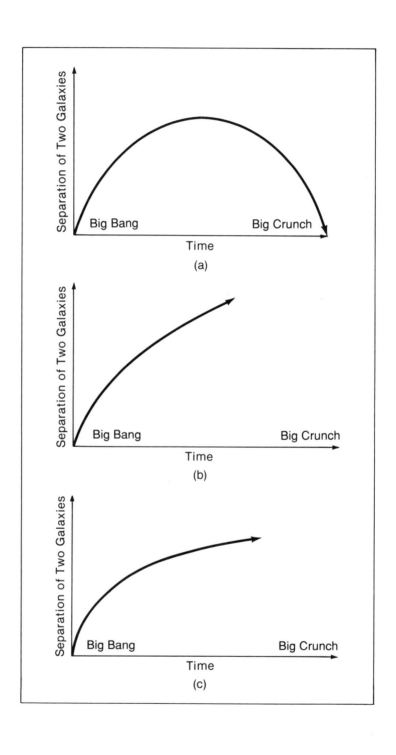

tually recollapses (Figure 4-6a)? Must that sort of universe also have begun as a singularity? By 1970 Hawking was able to show that it must have. He and Penrose wrote a joint paper proving that if the universe obeys general relativity and fits *any* of the Friedmann models, and if there's as much matter in the universe as we observe, the universe must have begun as a singularity, where all the mass of the universe was compressed to infinite density, where spacetime curvature was infinite, where the distance between all objects in the universe was zero.

Physical theories can't really work with infinite numbers. When the theory of general relativity predicts a singularity of infinite density and infinite spacetime curvature, it's also predicting its own breakdown. In fact, all our scientific theories break down at a singularity. We lose our ability to predict. We can't use the laws of physics to predict what would emerge from the singularity. It could be any sort of universe. And what about the question of what happened *before* the singularity? It's not even clear that this question has any meaning.

A singularity at the beginning of the universe would mean that the beginning of the universe is beyond our science, beyond anything that claims to be a Theory of Everything. We would simply have to say, time began, because we observe that it did, and that in itself is a very big arbitrary element. A singularity is a door slammed in our faces.

Figure 4-6. Three models that obey Friedmann's assumptions that (1) the universe looks much the same in any direction we look, and (2) the universe looks much the same from wherever you might be in the universe.

"Black hole explosions?"

"One evening in November of 1970, shortly after the birth of my daughter, Lucy, I started to think about black holes as I was getting into bed. My disability makes this rather a slow process, so I had plenty of time."[1]

The result of this thinking was a discovery so simple that with hindsight it seems anybody could have thought of it, but it was one which excited Hawking so much that he lay awake for most of the night. Penrose, Hawking insists, *had* thought of it but had not realized the implications.

The idea was that a black hole can never get smaller, because the area of an event horizon (the radius-of-no-return where escape velocity becomes greater than the speed of light) can never decrease.

To review briefly, a collapsing star reaches a radius where escape velocity is the speed of light. What happens to photons emitted by the star as it collapses past that radius? Gravity there is too strong to allow them to escape, but not strong enough to pull them into the black hole. They stay there, hovering. That radius is the event horizon. After that as the star continues to shrink, any photons it emits are drawn back in.

What Hawking realized was that the paths of light rays hovering at the event horizon cannot be paths of light rays that are approaching one another. Paths of light rays that approach one another would bash into one another and fall into the black hole, not hover. In order for the area of the event horizon to get smaller (and the black hole to get smaller), paths of light rays in the event horizon *would* have to approach one another. But, if they did, they would fall in, and the event horizon would still stay right where it had been all along, not get smaller.

Another way of thinking about this is to realize that a black hole *can* get *larger*. You learned in Chapter 4 that the size of a black hole is determined by its mass. So a black hole gets larger any time anything new falls in and adds to that mass. If nothing can get *out* of a black hole, its mass can't possibly decrease. A black hole can't get smaller.

Hawking's discovery became known as the second law of black hole dynamics: the area of the event horizon (the border of the black hole) can stay the same or increase but never decrease. If two or more black holes collide and form one black hole, the area of the new event horizon is as big as or bigger than the previous event horizons added together. A black hole can't get smaller or be destroyed or divided into two black holes, no matter how hard it might get zapped. Hawking's discovery reminded people of another familiar "second law" in physics: the second law of thermodynamics, which is about entropy.

Entropy is the amount of disorder there is in a system. We know that disorder always increases, never decreases. An assembled jigsaw puzzle put carefully in a box might get jostled, mixing the pieces and spoiling the picture. Nobody would be surprised if that happened. But it would be very surprising if any jostling of the box caused a mess of unassembled pieces to fall into place and complete the puzzle. In our universe entropy (disorder) always increases. Broken teacups never reassemble themselves. Your messy room never straightens itself up.

Suppose, however, you patch the teacup or clean your room. Something does become more ordered. Does entropy decrease? No. The mental and physical energy you burn in the process converts energy to a less useful form. That represents a decrease in the amount of order in the universe which outbalances any increase of order you achieved.

There's another way in which entropy resembles the event horizon of a black hole. When two systems join, the entropy of the combined system is as great as or greater than the entropy of the two systems added together. A familiar example describes gas molecules in a box. Think of them as little balls bouncing off one another and off the walls of the box. There's a partition down the center of the box. Half the box (one side of the partition) is filled with oxygen molecules. The other half is filled with nitrogen molecules. Remove the partition, and oxygen and nitrogen molecules start to mix. Soon there's a fairly uniform mixture throughout both halves of the box, but that's a less ordered state than when the partition was in place: Entropy—disorder—has increased. (The second law of thermodynamics doesn't always hold: There is the tiniest of chances, one in many millions of millions, that at some point the nitrogen molecules will be back in their half of the box and the oxygen molecules in the other.)

Suppose you toss the box of mixed-up molecules or anything else that has entropy into a convenient black hole. So much for that bit of entropy, you might think. The total amount of entropy outside the black hole is less than it was before. Have you managed to violate the second law? Someone might argue that the whole universe (inside and outside black holes) hasn't lost any entropy. But the fact is that anything going into a black hole is just plain lost to our universe. Or is it?

Escape from a Black Hole!

A graduate student at Princeton, Jacob Bekenstein, pointed out that you don't destroy entropy if you toss it into a black hole. The black hole already has entropy. You only increase it. In Bekenstein's way of thinking, the area of the event horizon of a black hole isn't only *like* entropy; it *is* entropy. When you measure the area of the event horizon, you're measuring the entropy of the black hole. When something falls into a black hole, such as a box of molecules, it adds to the mass of the black hole, and the event horizon gets larger. It also adds to the entropy of the black hole.

All of this brings us to a puzzling point. If something has entropy, it has a temperature. It isn't totally cold. If something has a temperature, it has to be radiating energy. If something is radiating energy, you can't say that nothing is coming out. Nothing was supposed to come out of black holes.

Hawking thought Bekenstein was mistaken. He was irritated by what he thought was Bekenstein's misuse of his discovery that event horizons never decrease. In 1972 he wrote a paper with two other physicists, James Bardeen and Brandon Carter, pointing out that although there were many similarities between entropy and the area of the event horizon, a black hole couldn't have entropy because it couldn't emit anything. It turned out they were wrong.

In 1962 when Hawking entered graduate school, he'd chosen to study cosmology, the study of the very large, rather than quantum mechanics, the study of the very small. Now, in 1973, he decided to shift ground and look at black holes through the eyes of quantum mechanics. It was the first serious, successful attempt by anybody to fuse the two great theories of the twentieth century: relativity and quantum mechanics. Such a fusion, you'll remember from Chapter 2, is a difficult hurdle on the road to a Theory of Everything.

In Moscow in 1973 Hawking spoke with two Soviet experts, Yakov Zel'dovich and Alexander Starobinskii. They convinced him that the uncertainty principle meant that rotating black holes would create and emit particles. Hawking wasn't satisfied with the way they calculated how much emission there should be. He proceeded to devise a better mathematical treatment.

Hawking expected his calculations to show that rotating black holes produce the radiation the Russians predicted. What he discovered was something far more dramatic: "I found, to my surprise and annoyance, that even nonrotating black holes should apparently create and emit particles at a steady rate."[2] At first he thought something had to be wrong with his calculations, and he spent many hours trying to find his error. He was particularly eager that Jacob Bekenstein not find out about his discovery and use it as an argument supporting his idea about event horizons and entropy. But the more Hawking thought about it, the more he had to admit that his calculations were certainly not far off the mark. The clincher was that the spectrum of the emitted particles was precisely what you'd expect from any hot body.

Bekenstein was right: You cannot make entropy decrease and the universe get more orderly by throwing matter carrying entropy into black holes as though they were great rubbish bins. As matter carrying entropy goes into a black hole, the area of the event horizon gets larger: the entropy of the black hole increases. The total entropy of the universe both inside and outside black holes hasn't become any less.

But how can black holes possibly have a temperature and emit particles if nothing can escape past the event horizon? Hawking found the answer in quantum mechanics.

When we think of space as a vacuum, we haven't got it quite right. You read in Chapter 2 that space is never a complete vacuum. Now we'll find out why.

The uncertainty principle means we can never know both the position and the velocity of a particle at the same time with complete accuracy. It means something more than that: we can never know both the value of a field (a gravitational field or an electromagnetic field, for instance) and the rate at which the field is changing over time with complete accuracy. The more precisely we know the value of a field, the less precisely we know the rate of change, and vice versa: the seesaw again. The upshot is that a field can never measure zero. Zero would be a very precise measurement of both the value of the field and its rate of change, and the uncertainty principle won't allow that. You don't have empty space unless all fields are exactly zero: no zero—no empty space.

Instead of the empty space, the true vacuum, that most of us assume is out there, we have a minimum amount of uncertainty, a bit of fuzziness, as to just what the value of a field is in "empty" space. You can think of this fluctuation in the value of the field, this wobbling a bit toward the positive and negative sides of zero so as never to *be* zero, in the following way:

Pairs of particles—pairs of photons or gravitons—continually appear. The two particles in a pair start out together then move apart. After an interval of time too short to imagine they come together again and annihilate one another—a short but eventful life. Quantum mechanics tells us this is happening all the time, every-where in the "vacuum" of space.

These may not be "real" particles that we can detect with a particle detector, but you mustn't get the idea that they're imaginary. Even if they are only "virtual" particles, we know they exist because we can measure their effects on other particles.

Some of the pairs will be pairs of *matter* particles, fermions. In this case, one of the pair is an antiparticle. "Antimatter," familiar from fantasy games and science fiction (it drives the starship *Enterprise*), isn't purely fictional.

You may have learned that the total amount of energy in the universe always stays the same. There cannot be any suddenly appearing from nowhere. How do we get around that rule with these newly created pairs? They're created by a very temporary "borrowing" of energy. Nothing permanent at all. One of the pair has positive energy. The other has negative energy. The two balance out. Nothing is added to the total energy of the universe.

Stephen Hawking reasoned that there will be many particle pairs popping up at the event horizon of a black hole. The way he pictures it, a pair of virtual particles appears. Before the pair meet again and annihilate, the one with negative energy crosses the event horizon into the black hole. Does that mean the positive energy partner must follow its unfortunate companion in order to meet and annihilate? No. The gravitational field at the event horizon of a black hole is strong enough to do an astounding thing to virtual particles, even those unfortunates with negative energy: It can change them from "virtual" to "real."

The transformation makes a remarkable difference to the pair. They are no longer obliged to find one another and annihilate. They can both live much longer, and separately. The particle with positive energy might fall into the black hole, too, of course, but it doesn't have to. It's free of the partnership. It can escape. To an observer at a distance it appears to come out of the black hole. In fact, it comes from just outside. Meanwhile, its partner has carried negative energy into the black hole (Figure 5-1).

The radiation that's emitted by black holes in this manner is now called Hawking radiation. And with Hawking radiation, his second famous discovery about black holes, Stephen Hawking showed that his first famous discovery, the second law of black hole dynamics (that the area of the event horizon can never decrease), doesn't always hold. Hawking radiation means that a black hole might get smaller and eventually evaporate entirely—a truly radical concept.

How does Hawking radiation make a black hole get smaller? As the black hole transforms virtual particles to real particles, it loses energy. How can this happen, if nothing escapes through the event horizon? How can it lose anything? It's rather a trick answer: When the particle with negative energy carries this *negative* energy into the black hole, that makes *less* energy in the black hole. Negative means "minus," which means less.

That's how Hawking radiation robs the black hole of energy. When something has less energy, it automatically has less mass. Remember Albert Einstein's equation, $E = mc^2$? The E stands for energy; the m is for mass; the c is for the speed of light. When the energy (on one side of the equal sign) grows less (as it is doing in the black hole), something on the other side of the equal sign grows less too. The speed of light (c) can't change. It must be the mass that grows less. So, when we say a black hole is robbed of energy we're also saying it's robbed of mass.

Keep this in mind and remember what Newton taught us about gravity: Any change in the mass of a body changes the amount of gravitational pull it exerts

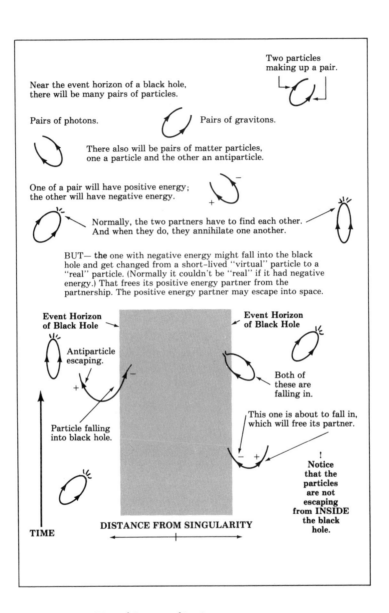

Near the event horizon of a black hole, there will be many pairs of particles.

Two particles making up a pair.

Pairs of photons.

Pairs of gravitons.

There also will be pairs of matter particles, one a particle and the other an antiparticle.

One of a pair will have positive energy; the other will have negative energy.

Normally, the two partners have to find each other. And when they do, they annihilate one another.

BUT— the one with negative energy might fall into the black hole and get changed from a short-lived "virtual" particle to a "real" particle. (Normally it couldn't be "real" if it had negative energy.) That frees its positive energy partner from the partnership. The positive energy partner may escape into space.

Event Horizon of Black Hole

Antiparticle escaping.

Particle falling into black hole.

Event Horizon of Black Hole

Both of these are falling in.

This one is about to fall in, which will free its partner.

!
Notice that the particles are not escaping from INSIDE the black hole.

TIME

DISTANCE FROM SINGULARITY

Figure 5-1. Hawking radiation

on another body. If the earth becomes less massive (not smaller this time, less massive), its gravitational pull feels weaker out where the moon is orbiting. If a black hole loses mass, its gravitational pull becomes weaker out where the event horizon (the radius-of-no-return) has been. Escape velocity at that radius becomes less than the speed of light. There is now a smaller radius where escape velocity is the speed of light. A new event horizon forms closer in. The event horizon has shrunk. This is the only way we know that a black hole can get smaller.

If we measure Hawking radiation from a large black hole, one resulting from the collapse of a star, we'll be disappointed. A black hole this size has a surface temperature of less than a millionth of a degree above absolute zero. The larger the black hole the lower the temperature. Stephen Hawking says, "Our ten-solar-mass black hole might emit a few thousand photons a second, but they would have a wavelength the size of the black hole and so little energy we would not be able to detect them."[3] The way it works is that the greater the mass, the greater the area of the event horizon. The greater the area of the event horizon, the greater the entropy. The greater the entropy, *the lower the surface temperature and the rate of emission.*

However, as early as 1971 Hawking suggested that there was a second type of black hole: tiny ones, the most interesting ones about the size of the nucleus of an atom. These would positively crackle with radiation. Recall that the smaller a black hole is, the hotter its surface temperature. Referring to these tiny black holes, Hawking declares, "Such holes hardly deserve [to be called] *black:* they really are *white hot.*"[4]

Primordial black holes, as Hawking calls them, don't form from the collapse of stars. They are relics of the very early universe. We might be able to make one ourselves if we could press matter together tightly enough. We can't, but in the very early universe there were pressures that could. Sometimes only a small amount of matter was compressed. In any case, a primordial black hole is by now much smaller even than it started out. It's been losing mass for a long time.

Hawking radiation has drastic consequences for a primordial black hole. As the mass grows less and the black hole gets smaller, the temperature and rate of emission of particles at the event horizon increase. The hole loses mass more and more quickly. The lower the mass, the higher the temperature—a vicious circle!

Nobody is sure how it ends. Hawking guesses that the little black hole disappears in a huge final puff of particle emission, like millions of hydrogen bombs exploding. Will a large black hole ever explode? The universe will come to an end long before it reaches that stage.

The idea that a black hole could get smaller and finally explode was so much the reverse of everything anybody thought about black holes in 1973 that Hawking had grave doubts about his discovery. For weeks he kept the idea under wraps, reviewing the calculations in his head. If he found it so hard to believe, it was fearful to predict what the rest of the scientific world would make of it. No scientist enjoys the prospect of ridicule. On the other hand, Hawking knew that if he were right, his idea would revolutionize astrophysics.

Hawking tested the idea on his close associates. The reception was mixed. A Cambridge physicist approached Hawking's old thesis supervisor, Denis Sciama, with the exclamation, "Have you heard? Stephen's changed everything!"[5] Sciama rallied to Hawking's support, urging him to release his findings.

Early in 1974 Hawking agreed to present his bizarre discovery in a paper at the Rutherford-Appleton Laboratory, south of Oxford. Traveling there, he still agonized over it. He'd hedged his bets a little by putting a question mark in the title, "Black Hole Explosions?"

The short presentation, including slides of equations, was greeted with embarrassed silence and few questions. Hawking's arguments had gone over the heads of many in the audience, experts in other fields. But it was more or less obvious to everyone that he was proposing something completely contrary to accepted theory. Those who did understand were shocked and unprepared to argue with him. The lights were snapped back on. The moderator, a respected professor from the University of London, rose and declared, "Sorry, Stephen, but this is absolute rubbish."[6]

Hawking published this "rubbish" the next month in the prestigious British science magazine *Nature*, and within days physicists were discussing it all over the world. A few called it the most significant discovery in theoretical physics in years. Sciama said the paper was "one of the most beautiful in the history of physics."[7] Things were looking up. Hawking had used the activity of virtual particles to explain about something that had arisen from the theory of relativity: black holes. He'd taken a step toward linking relativity and quantum physics.

1970–1974

Four years after the Hawkings bought and fixed up the house in Little Saint Mary's Lane, Stephen Hawking could no longer go up and down the stairs. Fortunately he was becoming an important physicist, and Caius College was now more helpful with housing. They offered the Hawkings a spacious ground-floor flat in a college-owned brick mansion on West Road, not far from the back gate of King's College. It had high ceilings and large windows and required only a little modification to make it more convenient for a wheelchair. Except for a gravel parking area in front, the house was surrounded by gardens tended by college gardeners. It was an ideal childhood home for the Hawking children.

The journey to the DAMTP took about ten minutes by a wide footpath across the "Backs"—the meadows, shady lawns, and gardens along the River Cam—then across the river and through the historic center of Cambridge. In the early 1970s Stephen Hawking was making the trip in a wheelchair. He'd lost the battle to stay on his feet. Friends watched with sadness, but Hawking's humor and strength of purpose didn't fail him.

Stephen and Jane Hawking continued to keep his illness in the background of their lives and not allow it to become the most important thing about him or about them. They made a habit of not looking to the future. As far as the rest of the world could see, they succeeded so well that it comes as a surprise to hear Jane Hawking speak of how terrible the difficulties sometimes were. Discussing all the honors that have come her husband's way, she says, "I wouldn't say [this overwhelming success makes] all the blackness worthwhile. I don't think I am ever going to reconcile in my mind the swings of the pendulum we have experienced from the depths of a black hole to the heights of all the glittering prizes."[8] To judge from everything Stephen Hawking has written, he's barely noticed the depths. It may be that talking about them in any but the most offhand manner, which is the most he allows himself, would be for him a form of giving in, of defeat, and would undermine his resolute disregard of his problems.

Jane Hawking worked hard to meet the needs of her growing family and her wheelchair-bound husband. She devoted all her time and energy to encouraging him, keeping his life completely normal in spite of his worsening condition, making it possible for him to continue his work, and at the same time ensuring that Robert and Lucy weren't robbed of a normal childhood. Until 1974 she managed single-handedly: nursing him, caring for the children, and keeping house with no outside help.

Speaking in the late eighties, Jane Hawking attributed her ability to cope with all this for so many years to her faith in God. Without that, she said, "I wouldn't have been able to live in this situation. I wouldn't have been able to marry Stephen in the first place, because I wouldn't have had the optimism to carry me through, and I wouldn't be able to carry on with it."[9]

The faith which supported her so magnificently was not shared by her husband. If there's been a religious or philosophical side to Stephen Hawking's confrontation with disability and the threat of early death, he's never spoken about that publicly. However, it seems evident from his book *A Brief History of Time* that God is never far from Hawking's mind. He told an interviewer, "It is difficult to discuss the beginning of the universe without mentioning the concept of God. My work on the origin of the universe is on the borderline between science and religion, but I try to stay [on the scientific] side of the border. It is quite possible that God acts in ways that cannot be described by scientific laws. But in that case one would just have to go by personal belief."[10] Asked whether he thinks his science is in competition with religion, he answers, "If one took that attitude, then Newton [who was a very religious man] would not have discovered the law of gravity."[11]

Hawking isn't an atheist, but he prefers to "use the term God as the embodiment of the laws of physics." "We are such insignificant creatures on a minor planet of a very average star in the outer suburbs of one of a hundred thousand million galaxies. So it is difficult to believe in a God that would care about us or even notice our existence."[12] Einstein shared Hawking's view. Others would agree with Jane Hawking and call this a rather limited view of God and point out that it's equally difficult to believe that all the intelligent and rational people (many scientists among them) who say they have experienced a personal God are somehow deluded. They would paraphrase a famous Hawking quote, "If it isn't

85

[God], it's *really* something exotic!"[13] And just how *are* we to explain it? Whatever the answer, this enormous difference in outlook could hardly be illustrated more strikingly than in the views of Stephen and Jane Hawking.

"I used to find Stephen's assertion that he doesn't believe in a personal God quite hurtful,"[14] Jane remembers. She told an interviewer in 1988, "He is delving into realms that really do matter to thinking people and in a way that can have a very disturbing effect on people.[15] There's one aspect of his thought that I find increasingly upsetting and difficult to live with. It's the feeling that, because everything is reduced to a rational, mathematical formula, that must be the truth."[16] It seemed to her that there was no room in her husband's mind for the possibility that the truth revealed in his mathematics might not be the whole truth. A year later she had changed her outlook somewhat: "As one grows older it's easier to take a broader view. I think the whole picture for him is so different from the whole picture for anybody else by virtue of his condition and his circumstances . . . being an almost totally paralyzed genius . . . that nobody else can understand what his view of God or what his relationship with God might be."[17]

6

"Was it all just a lucky chance?"

1974–1983

In the late 1960s it might have seemed generous, keeping on a young physicist who hadn't long to live, who would probably contribute little to his department in terms of lecturing and teaching. By the mid-1970s Hawking's university and department had begun to realize that they'd done themselves a favor. He'd become a considerable asset.

At Cambridge extraordinary minds and personalities aren't uncommon. They crop up in one university department or another on a regular basis. It's a healthy environment for genius. No matter how much one is treated with awe in the wider world, within the university community it's usually just business as usual. The DAMTP had from the beginning exempted Hawking from heavy teaching duties and allowed him to concentrate on his research and a few seminars and graduate students. However, even in the late 1970s, when he'd become something of a legend, he and all his specialized equipment—gadgets to turn pages for him, computer terminals with special controls so that he could use them like a blackboard—still shared a cramped office with another researcher.

Awareness of the needs of disabled people and the possibility that they might expect to live normal, even brilliantly successful and active, lives was not so much a part of our culture in the 1970s as it is becoming today. Only after a lengthy bureaucratic dispute about who should pay for it was a ramp for Hawking's wheelchair installed into the DAMTP building. Hawking fought and won other battles for wheelchair access in Cambridge. Where there was no such access, anyone near at hand was likely to be conscripted to lift Hawking and his chair up and down stairs.

Until 1974 Hawking could still feed himself and get into and out of bed. But as such actions became increasingly difficult, the Hawkings finally decided they couldn't go on managing alone. They began a custom of asking one of his research students to live with them. In return for free accommodation and extra attention from Hawking, the student helped him get ready for bed and get up.

Jane Hawking remembers that being unable to assist with his children or play with them in an active way was difficult for Hawking. She taught them to play cricket ("I can get them out!" she gloated), and she teased her husband that, unlike other wives, she was not surprised or disillusioned when he proved useless around the house and with the children.

Hawking's practical uselessness became one of the positive side effects of his illness. It may take him a long time to get up and go to bed, but he doesn't have to run errands, do home repairs, mow the grass, make travel arrangements, pack his suitcase, draw up lecture schedules, or serve in time-consuming administrative positions in the DAMTP or at Caius. Such matters are left to Hawking's colleagues and assistants and to his wife. He can spend all his time thinking about physics, a luxury which his colleagues envy him.

An overwhelming proportion of these day-to-day responsibilities fell to Jane Hawking. Anticipating this, she had decided even before they were married in the 1960s that only one of them would be able to have a career, and it would have to be her husband. In the 1970s, perhaps partly because attitudes about the role of women were changing, that sacrifice became more difficult for her to accept. She'd thought that giving her ailing husband the encouragement and assistance he so badly needed would give her life purpose and meaning. What it was not giving her was an identity. Motherhood wasn't exactly doing that either. As she puts it, although she adores her children and "would not have wanted to farm them out to anybody else, Cambridge is a jolly difficult place to live if your only identity is as the mother of small children."[1]

To be fair to the university community, whenever you mention the name Hawking in Cambridge someone is likely to comment that Jane Hawking is even more remarkable than Stephen. However, in the 1970s, Jane Hawking didn't feel that was her reputation. As she saw it, in Cambridge "the pressure is on you to make your way academically."[2] She decided to go back to school to earn a Ph.D. in medieval languages from Cambridge. Degree in hand she became a teacher at the high-school level. "It is fulfilling a part of me," she said, "that I feel has been suppressed for a long time and the marvellous thing is that it is totally compatible with what goes on at home."[3]

Robert, Lucy, and later Timmy, who was born in 1979, were favorites at their neighborhood grade school. The first I ever heard of any of the Hawkings was a comment from the head teacher that my daughter (a first-grade student there in the mid-1980s) reminded her of Lucy Hawking. This was obviously meant as a compliment. Later when I met Lucy (then fifteen), who was helping with the small children on the playground, I found that it was. Lucy is a radiant, clean-cut blonde, brimming with intelligence and personality, with a thoughtfulness and composure beyond her years. She says she's not like her father. "I was never any good at science. I even managed to be hopeless at maths as well, which was slightly embarrassing."[4] But she's actually a fine student and cellist. It's unlikely anyone has ever wagered a bag of candy against her success or that of her brothers.

Jane Hawking had much to be proud of in the 1970s. Robert and Lucy were turning out well; Hawking's career as a physicist was skyrocketing; his reputation as a remarkably tough and good-humored man when the odds were against him was becoming legendary; and she was making her own mark academically. At the same time she felt increasingly that her enormous and burdensome role in Hawking's success went largely unnoticed. Hers was a problem which is not unusual for persons with a talent for making things look easy: Others begin to assume that things *are* easy for them and fail to appreciate the sacrifice and effort involved. Both Jane Hawking and her husband knew that none of his success—probably not even his survival—could have happened without her. But she was allowed to share little of the triumph, nor could she follow his mathematical reasoning and share his pleasure in that. Nevertheless, media accounts which make much of her feeling unappreciated are a bad distortion of the truth. "The joy and excitement of Stephen's success were tremendous,"[5] she says. She remembers those years with happiness, and does not regret the decision she made to marry him. However, the rewards "didn't alleviate the heartrending difficulties of coping day after day with motor neurone disease."[6]

There were, however, many pleasures the Hawkings shared. They loved classical music and attended concerts and the theater together. At Christmas they took the children to the pantomime. They also loved entertaining. Don Page, who as a postgraduate researcher lived with the Hawkings for three years as Hawking's assistant, remembers that Jane Hawking was "very outgoing . . . a great professional asset" to her husband.[7] It wasn't unheard of to find her in the market shopping for a party of sixty people. The Hawkings became reknowned for their hospitality.

Earlier in the 1970s it was still possible to carry on a normal conversation with Hawking. However, by the late 1970s and early 1980s, his speech was so slurred that only his family and closest friends could understand him. The job of "interpreter" frequently fell to the research student who currently lived with them. Michael Harwood, who interviewed Hawking for *The New York Times*, describes the process: "Don Page, sitting beside him, leans close to hear the indistinct words, mouths each phrase to be certain he has caught it, often pauses and asks for a repetition, speaks a phrase back to Hawking sometimes to make certain, corrects himself."[8] Another interviewer recalls that he often thought Hawking had finished a sentence only to find with the "interpretation" that he'd spoken just one word. Hawking wrote his scientific papers by dictating them in this tedious fashion to his secretary. But he was learning to state ideas in the fewest words possible and to get to the point in scientific papers and conversations. What he was saying in those few words was receiving worldwide attention.

The procession of awards and recognition that continues to the present began soon after Hawking announced his discovery of exploding black holes. In 1974 he was inducted into the Royal Society, one of the world's most prestigious bodies of scientists. At thirty-two he was young for the honor. During the rite of investiture, a ceremony dating from the seventeenth century, new Fellows walk to the podium to write their names in the book, the earliest pages of which contain the signature of Isaac Newton. Those present when Hawking was inducted remember that the president of the society, Sir Alan Hodgkin, Nobel prize winner in biology, broke tradition and carried the book down to Hawking in the front row. Hawking could still write his name with great effort, but it took him a long time. The gathering of eminent scientists waited respectfully. When Hawking finished and looked up with a broad grin, they gave him an ovation.

Internationally Hawking's reputation flourished. He was invited to spend a year at California Institute of Technology as Sherman Fairchild Distinguished Scholar. Jane Hawking scheduled air flights, packed, and moved belongings, two small children, husband, and specialized equipment across the world to southern California and back with efficiency that awed her friends. Lucy and Robert visited Disneyland.

The honors kept coming: six major international awards and six honorary doctorates in the late 1970s and early 1980s, including the coveted Albert Einstein Award in America and an honorary degree from his alma mater, Oxford. Queen Elizabeth named him a "Commander of the British Empire," allowing him to put "CBE" after his name.

In 1979, when Cambridge University gave Hawking the prestigious title of Lucasian Professor of Mathematics, he at last got a private office.

The Elusive Moment of Creation

In the 1970s Hawking's primary interest was black holes. In 1981 he turned his attention once again to the question of how the universe began and how it would end. At a conference at the Vatican that year, the pope warned Hawking and other scientists that humans shouldn't inquire into the moment of Creation: that was the work of

God. At the same conference Hawking proposed the possibility that there was no "beginning," no "boundaries" for the universe. Did that mean there was no "Creation"? Or was Hawking's idea possibly consistent with the Judeo-Christian concept of a God existing outside time—the "I Am" of the Bible—for whom it is believed there is no beginning, no end, nor anything like our chronological time, but for whom everything happens simultaneously? An entirely new way of looking at time was to be a major part of Hawking's "no-boundary proposal."

The work Hawking had done in the late 1960s, in his Ph.D. dissertation and afterward, seemed to prove that the universe had begun as a singularity, a point of infinite density and infinite spacetime curvature. At that singularity all our laws of physics would break down, and it would be useless, regardless of whether the pope approved, to try to investigate the moment of creation. Any sort of universe could come out of a singularity. There would certainly be no way to predict that it would be a universe just like ours. In fact, Hawking told John Boslough in the early 1980s, "The odds against a universe like ours emerging out of something like the Big Bang are enormous. I think there are clearly religious implications whenever you start to discuss the origins of the universe."[9]

The "Anthropic Principle"

Most of us have become convinced that the sun, the planets, and everything else don't revolve around the earth. Science also tells us that the universe probably looks the same from any vantage point. Earth, with us as its favored passengers, isn't the center of everything.

Nevertheless, the more we discover on both the microscopic and the cosmic levels, the more we're struck with the impression that some careful planning, some incredible fine-tuning, had to occur to make the universe a place where it's possible for us to exist. In the early 1980s Hawking was saying, "If one considers the possible constants and laws that could have emerged, the odds against a universe that has produced life like ours are immense."[10]

There are many examples of this mysterious fine-tuning: Hawking points out that if the electric charge of the electron had been slightly different, stars either wouldn't burn to give us light or wouldn't have exploded in supernovas to fling back into space the raw material for new stars like our sun or planets like earth. If gravity were less powerful than it is, matter couldn't have congealed into stars and galaxies, nor could galaxies and solar systems have formed had gravity not been at the same time the *weakest* of the four forces. No theory we have at present can predict the strength of gravity or the electric charge of the electron. These are arbitrary elements, discoverable only by observation, but they seem minutely adjusted to make possible the development of life as we know it.

Shall we jump to the conclusion that Someone or Something had us in mind when things were set up? Is the universe, as the astronomer Fred Hoyle phrased it, "a put up job," a great conspiracy to make intelligent life possible? Or are we missing other possible explanations?

"We see the universe the way it is because we exist." "Things are as they are because we are." "If it had been different we wouldn't be here to notice it." All of these are ways of stating something called the anthropic principle.

Hawking explains the anthropic principle as follows: Picture a lot of different, separate universes, or different regions of the same universe. The conditions in most of these universes, or in these regions of the same universe, will not allow the development of intelligent life. However, in a very few of them, the conditions will be just right for stars and galaxies and solar systems to form and for intelligent beings to develop and study the universe and ask the question, Why is the universe as we observe it? According to the anthropic principle, the only answer to their question may be that, if it were otherwise, there wouldn't be anybody around to ask the question.

Does the anthropic principle really explain anything? Some scientists say that it doesn't, but it certainly does show how what seems like fine-tuning might instead be a random bit of good luck. It's like the old story about giving enough monkeys typewriters so that by the laws of chance one of them would type the first line of the Gettysburg Address. Even if our sort of universe is highly unlikely, with enough universes around, one of them might very well be like ours.

Does the anthropic principle rule out God? No. However, it does show that the universe could appear tailor-made for our good without there being a God.

John Wheeler thinks we might carry the anthropic principle a step further. Perhaps, he suggests, there can be no physical laws at all unless there are observers to figure them out. In that case there won't be all those alternate universes, because any universe that didn't allow for the development of observers simply wouldn't exist.

If this is so, does it mean that if we become extinct, so will the universe? Will the stage crew come out and dismantle the set as the last member of the audience leaves the theater? In fact, if we're not around to remember that it existed, will it ever have existed? Or does our having observed a brief slice of its existence give it the power to go on existing after we're gone?

A few physicists like to make a connection between an observer-dependent universe and some of the ideas in Eastern mysticism: Hinduism, Buddhism, and Taoism. They get no encouragement from Hawking, who says, "The universe of Eastern mysticism is an illusion. A physicist who attempts to link it with his own work has abandoned physics."[11]

Although he didn't invent the idea, the anthropic principle is often associated with Hawking, along with Brandon Carter and other colleagues. However, Hawking and most other physicists hope we won't have to turn to it as the only explanation for why we have the sort of universe we have and not another. "Was it all just a lucky chance?" Hawking asks. "That would seem a counsel of despair, a negation of all our hopes of understanding the underlying order of the universe."[12] The pope had warned him off; the anthropic principle said it was just a roll of the dice (one roll among an almost infinite number) that fell in our favor. Some were arguing that God had the power to change His mind and adjust things, including the laws of the universe, whenever He pleased. But Hawking didn't think an all-powerful God would have any need to change his mind. He believed there are laws that held at the time that we call the beginning, or the Creation—that made our universe the way it is and not some other way—and that we are capable of understanding them. He wanted to know what those laws are. That meant that somehow he had to cut the ultimate Gordian knot: the singularity.

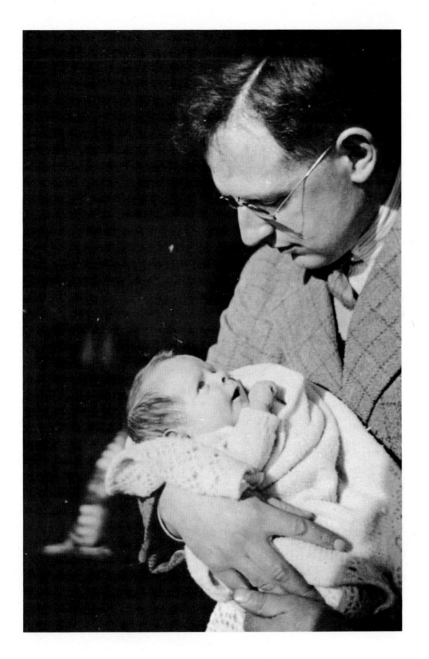

Dr. Frank Hawking with his newborn son,
Stephen, January 1942

(Above) Stephen and his sister Mary at the seashore
(Below) Stephen with his new bicycle looks
very likely to amount to "something" despite
his schoolfriend's bet that he won't.

Stephen at the helm

(Above) Saint Alban's school, where Stephen attended secondary school. (Below) Hawking and friends enjoy the good life at Oxford during the early 1960's.

Hawking, age twenty, upon graduation with
First Class Honors (just barely) from Oxford in 1962

(Above) Hawking, with his mother
Isobel Hawking (left) in the mid-1960s
(Below) Hawking with newborn son,
Robert, in the late 1960s

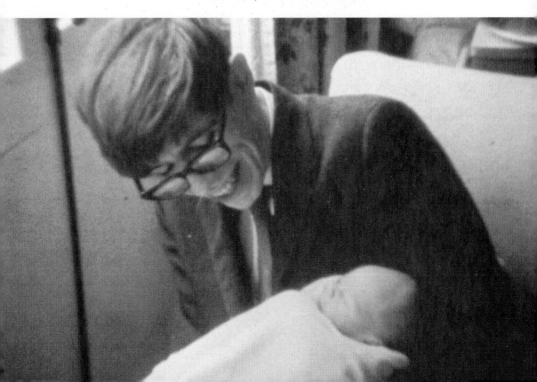

(Above) The Hawkings moved to this house in West Road, Cambridge, in the early 1970's. (Below) Department of Applied Mathematics and Theoretical Physics, Cambridge University. Hawking's office is on the ground floor in the wing to the right.

Whereas Stephen Hawking
has such a large investment in
General Relativity and Black
Holes and desires an insurance
policy, and whereas Kip Thorne likes
to live dangerously without an
insurance policy,
    Therefore be it resolved that
Stephen Hawking bets 1 year's
subscription to "Penthouse" as against
Kip Thorne's wager of a 4-year
subscription to "Private Eye", that
Cygnus X 1 does not contain a
black hole of mass above the
Chandrasekhar limit.

Kip S. Thorne

Witnessed this tenth
day of December 1974.
Hrindman Anna Zytkow Werner Jr

Black hole wager. This famous bet, made in 1974, was
finally paid off in 1990. American physicist Kip Thorne
insists it still isn't certain whether Cygnus X-1 is a black
hole. Hawking, however, secretly entered Thorne's office
at the California Institute of Technology and attached
to this document a note in which he conceded the bet.

(Above) Hawking at age thirty-seven in 1979. He would soon make his prediction that the "theory of everything" might be discovered before the end of the century. (Below) Don Page (center) "interprets" as Hawking converses with a visitor. By the late 1970s, Hawking's speech had deteriorated to such a degree that only those who knew him well could understand him.

(Left top) Hawking's children Timmy and Lucy play in
the sandbox behind their house. Stephen Hawking, his
wife, Jane, and oldest son, Robert, look on in this photo
taken early in the 1980's. (Left bottom) In Hawking's study
son Timmy, perched on his father's lap, is about to
lose an arm down a black hole, with a little help from
his brother Robert. The model held by Robert shows
how a black hole curves spacetime. (Above) Hawking
with his wife, Jane, and daughter, Lucy in the sitting
room of their house in West Road, in 1988.

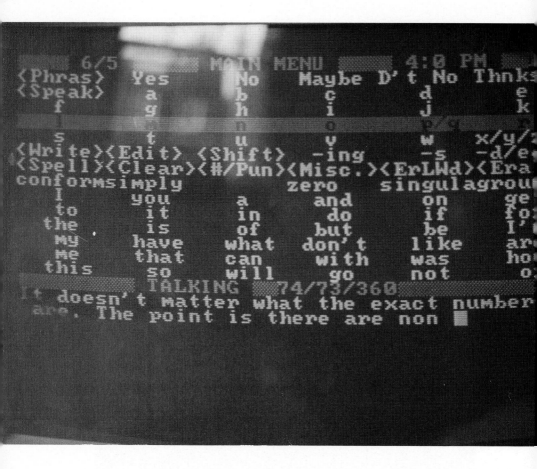

(Above) Hawking communicates via this computer screen. As he scans the words and chooses those he needs to build a sentence, they appear across the lower portion of the screen.

(Top right) In his office, Hawking converses with his postgraduate assistant Raymond Laflamme. When visitors and students come to see Hawking, they sit beside him in order to read his computer screen.

(Bottom right) A familiar figure in the streets and courts of Cambridge, Hawking is usually accompanied by a nurse, and often by a flock of students.

IN *the chapel of Trinity College stands the figure of Isaac Newton,*

> *The marble index of a mind forever*
> *Voyaging through strange seas of thought alone.*

Here is the present heir to Newton's title, embarked on a voyage of equal ambition, into the infinities of space and time. He first turned his thoughts to the galaxies, where a star in its death throes, its fuel exhausted, collapses to a point of matter infinitesimal in size, yet in mass so dense, in gravity so powerful, that not even light can escape. He has plumbed with mathematics the mysteries of these Black Holes, and discovered what radiation is generated at their surfaces, what power these invisible ghostly voids exert on the visible universe. From the vast spaces where stars live and die with predictability, he has travelled to the subatomic world, where elementary particles obey a contrary law, the law of uncertainty. To reconcile the laws which relate to phenomena on the largest scale, the gravitational laws of Newton and the relativity of Einstein, with the law which relates to the small, the uncertainty principle of quantum mechanics, and in so doing to devise a new and unified theory which will explain the nature and behaviour of all matter, how the universe came into being, and how it developed, and how it may end, is today the greatest intellectual challenge of theoretical science. And in the pursuit of this goal he is the standard-bearer and guide. Fired by a passion to communicate, he has encapsulated in one slim volume's best-selling pages, with a limpid style and engaging wit, a whole Brief History of Time.

I present to you

STEPHEN WILLIAM HAWKING, C.B.E., PH.D.,

Fellow of Gonville and Caius College, Honorary Fellow of Trinity Hall, Lucasian Professor of Mathematics.

(Above) A flamboyant summing-up of Hawking's achievements. This is the English translation of a Latin oration given when Hawking was awarded an honorary degree from Cambridge University. (Right) Presenting a lecture on baby universes at Northeastern University in Boston. All over the world, fans line up hours in advance to gain admittance to Hawking's public lectures

Stephen Hawking nearing age fifty, in the early
1990s. "I have been lucky," he says, "but it
shows that one need not lose hope."

**"In all my travels,
I have not managed to fall off
the edge of the world."**

In 1974 Hawking's suggestion that black holes emit radiation was greeted at first with skepticism, but we've seen that most physicists soon came to agree it wasn't nonsense after all. Black holes must radiate as any hot body does if our other ideas about general relativity and quantum mechanics aren't badly off base. No one has found a primordial black hole yet, but if one were discovered, physicists would be shocked to find it *not* emitting a shower of gamma rays and X rays.

Go back to thinking about the particles that are emitted by a black hole in Hawking radiation. A pair of particles appears at the event horizon. The particle with negative energy falls into the black hole. The fact that its energy is negative means we have energy subtracted from the black hole. What happens to that energy? (We don't think energy can simply disappear from the universe.) It is carried off into space with the positive energy particle (see Chapter 5).

The upshot, you'll remember, is that the black hole loses mass and its event horizon shrinks. For a primordial black hole the whole story may end with the black hole's disappearing completely, probably with an impressive fireworks display. The matter that was pressed together to form the black hole, and any other matter that fell in, hasn't disappeared from the universe. It's been neatly recycled as Hawking radiation. How can something escape from a black hole if nothing can escape from a black hole? It really is one of the great "locked room mysteries" of all time, solved by "S. H."

If Hawking was correct in 1974 and matter in a black hole doesn't necessarily reach the absolute end of time at a singularity, doesn't that raise suspicions about another singularity: the singularity he had decided earlier was at the absolute *beginning* of time?

With that question in mind in 1981 Hawking was back in the early universe. Quantum theory offered a fresh possibility: Maybe the Big Bang singularity is, as he terms it, "smeared away." Maybe the door isn't slammed in our faces after all.

Hawking points to a similar problem which quantum theory solved early in our century, a problem related to Rutherford's model of the atom: "There was a problem with the structure of the atom, which was supposed to consist of a number of electrons orbiting around the central nucleus, like the planets around the Sun" [see Figure 2-1]. "The previous classical theory predicted that each electron would radiate light waves because of its motion. The waves would carry away energy and so would cause the electrons to spiral inwards until they collided with the nucleus."[1] Something had to be wrong with this picture, because atoms *don't* collapse in this manner.

Quantum mechanics, with the uncertainty principle, came to the rescue. You've learned that, because of the uncertainty principle, you can't know simultaneously both a definite position and a definite velocity for an electron. "If an electron were to sit on the nucleus, it would have both a definite position and a definite velocity," Hawking points out. "Instead, quantum mechanics predicts that the electron does not have a definite position but that the probability of finding it is spread out over some region around the nucleus." The electrons don't spiral inward and hit the nucleus. Atoms don't collapse.

According to Hawking, "The prediction of classical theory [that we will find the electrons at the nucleus] is rather similar to the prediction of classical general relativity that there should be a Big Bang singularity of infinite density."[2] Knowing that everything is at one point of infinite density at the Big Bang or in a black hole is too precise a measurement to be allowed by the uncertainty principle. To Hawking's way of thinking this principle should "smear out" the singularities predicted by general relativity, just as it smeared out the positions of electrons. There is no collapse of the atom, and he suspected that there was no singularity at the beginning of the universe or inside a black hole. Space would be very compressed there, but probably not to a point of infinite density.

The theory of general relativity had predicted that inside a black hole and at the Big Bang the curvature of spacetime becomes infinite. If that *doesn't* happen, then Hawking wanted to figure out "what shape space and time may adopt instead of the point of infinite curvature."[3]

When Time Is Time and Space Is Space

If you find the following discussion difficult, don't hesitate to skim over it. It isn't necessary to understand every word to appreciate Hawking's theory, but it's more interesting if you can. Of course, the math Hawking uses to describe it, and that you and I would need in order to understand him completely, is much more complicated than the simple math you will find here.

Relativity theory links space and time in four-dimensional spacetime: three dimensions of space and one of time. Take a look at what a spacetime diagram is like. Here's one showing a girl named Caitlin on her way from her classroom to the lunchroom. The vertical line on the left represents the passage of time. The horizontal line at the bottom represents all the space dimensions. Any single point on our spacetime diagram represents a position in space and a moment in time. Let's see how this works.

The diagram (Figure 7-1) begins with Caitlin at her desk in her classroom, at 12:00 noon. She sits still, moving forward in time but going nowhere in space. On the diagram a little band of "Caitlin" moves forward in time. At 12:05 the bell rings. Caitlin moves toward the lunchroom. (Her desk still moves forward in time but goes nowhere in space.) Caitlin moves in both time and space. At 12:07 she pauses to retie her sneaker. For one minute she moves forward in time but does not move in space. At 12:08 she's off again toward the lunchroom, walking a little faster than before so she won't be last in line. At 12:15 she arrives at the lunchroom. A physicist would say we have traced Caitlin's "world-line."

That spacetime diagram was a very sketchy affair. When physicists draw a spacetime diagram, they often use a common unit for both space and time. They might, for instance, use one yard as the unit of both space and time. (One yard of time is very small, only billionths of a second. It's the time it takes a photon, which moves at the speed of light, to travel one yard.) In such a spacetime diagram, if something moves four yards in space and four yards in time, its world-line traces a 45-degree angle. That's the world-line for something moving at the speed of light, a photon, for instance (Figure 7-2). If

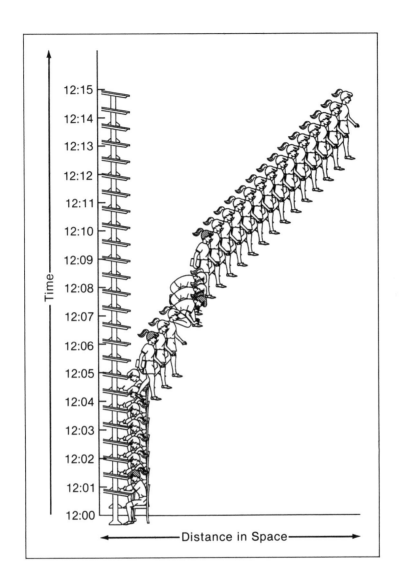

*Figure 7-1. Caitlin
in spacetime*

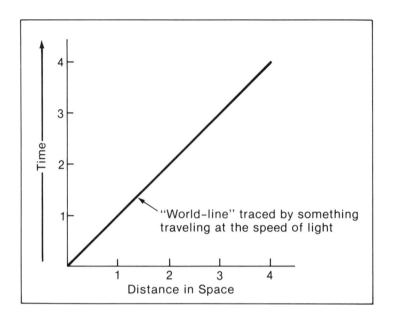

Figure 7-2. A spacetime diagram using one yard as the unit of both space and time. If something travels four yards in space and four yards in time, its "world-line" traces a 45-degree angle on a spacetime diagram. That's the world-line for a photon, or anything else moving at the speed of light.

something moves three yards in space and four in time, it's moving at three-fourths the speed of light (Figure 7-3a). If something moves four yards in space and three in time, it's exceeding the speed of light, which isn't allowed (Figure 7-3b).

The next diagram (Figure 7-4) shows two events happening simultaneously. They have no way of knowing about each other at the instant they happen because, for them to do so, the information would have to have a

102

world-line running at a 90-degree angle from the time-line. Traveling such a world-line would require faster-than-light travel. Nothing can travel faster than light and light can't manage anything greater than a 45-degree angle on the diagram.

Now we'll talk about the "length" of a world-line. How shall we say what the length of a world-line is—a length that takes into account all four dimensions?

Let's examine the world-line of something that moves faster than Caitlin. The object in Figure 7-5 moves four yards in space and five in time: four-fifths the speed of light. Think of the distance it moves in the "space" direction on the diagram as one side of a triangle (side A). Think of the distance it moves in the "time" direction on the diagram as a second side (side B). That makes two sides of a right triangle. The world-line of the moving object is the hypotenuse of that triangle (side C).

Most of you have learned that the square of the hypotenuse of a right triangle is equal to the sum of the squares of the other two sides. The square of 4 (side A) is 16. The square of 5 (side B) is 25. The sum of 16 and 25 is 41. The length of side C, the hypotenuse, would be the square root of 41.

That's the way it works in our familiar school geometry. For spacetime it's a little different. The square of the hypotenuse (side C) is not equal to the *sum* of the squares of the other two sides. It's equal to the *difference between* the squares of the two other sides. Our object travels four yards in space (side A of the triangle) and five yards in time (side B). The square of 4 is 16; the square of 5 is 25. The difference between 25 and 16 is 9. The square root of 9 is 3. So we know that the third side of the triangle, side C, the world-line of our traveling object, is three yards in length in spacetime.

Let's say, just for the fun of it, that the object is someone wearing a watch. The watch will show that

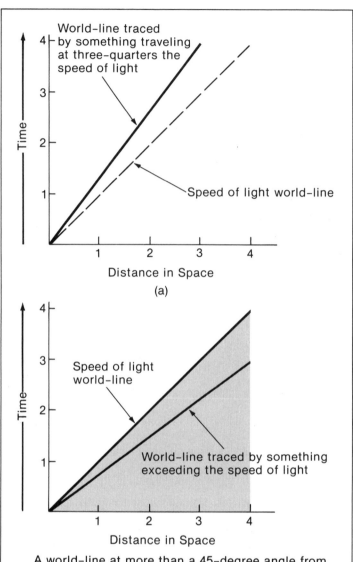

World-line traced by something traveling at three-quarters the speed of light

Speed of light world-line

Time

Distance in Space

1   2   3   4

(a)

Time

Speed of light world-line

World-line traced by something exceeding the speed of light

Distance in Space

1   2   3   4

A world-line at more than a 45-degree angle from the time-line, like this one, is not allowed. That's the same as saying that world-lines beginning at zero on the space-line and moving through the shaded area are not allowed. Tracing such a world-line would require faster-than-light travel.

(b)

length (three yards) as "time." In Figure 7-6 Lauren remains stationary in space and measures five hours on her watch. Her twin brother Tim, moving at four-fifths the speed of light, meanwhile measures only three hours on his. Tim turns around and returns, again measuring three hours while Lauren measures five. Tim's slightly younger than Lauren when next they meet. This is one of the remarkable, unbelievable things that Einstein taught us about the universe.

Now let's consider spacetime diagrams and world-lines of some smaller objects, elementary particles.

"Sums-Over Histories" or The Likelihood of Visiting Venus

Remember the smeared-out positions of electrons in the model of the atom we talked about earlier. Their positions were smeared out because we couldn't measure simultaneously both the position and the velocity of any one of them very precisely. Richard Feynman, the American physicist, had a way of dealing with this problem which we now call "sums-over-histories."

Imagine that you are considering all the different

Figure 7-3. (A) A spacetime diagram showing the world-line traced by something moving three yards in space and four yards in time: three-quarters the speed of light. (B) World-line traced by something moving four yards in space and three yards in time. When the distance traveled is greater in space than in time, as in this case, the object is exceeding the speed of light (not allowed!).

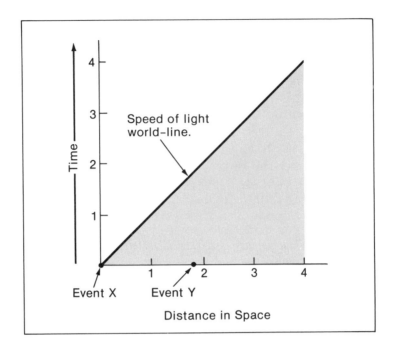

Figure 7-4. A spacetime diagram showing two events (X and Y) that occur simultaneously but at a distance from each other in space. They can't know about each other at the exact moment they occur, because any information traveling from one to the other must have a world-line running at less than a 45-degree angle from the time-line. A world-line running at greater than a 45-degree angle requires faster-than-light travel. That's not allowed in our universe.

routes you might take home from school—not just the quickest way as the crow flies or the safest route by bicycle, but every possible route you might take. There are billions and billions of possible routes. You ultimately get a gigantic fuzzy picture of yourself coming home by all these possible routes at once. However, some are certainly more likely than others. If you study the probabilities of your taking the various routes, you conclude that you're very unlikely at any time between school and home to be found on the planet Venus, for instance.

In a similar manner, with sums-over-histories, physicists figure every possible path in spacetime that could have been traveled by a certain particle, all the possible "histories" the particle could have had. It's possible then to figure the *probability* of a particle's having passed through a particular point, something like figuring how likely you are to come home by way of the planet Venus. (You don't want to get the idea, however, that particles *choose* a path. That would be carrying the analogy too far.)

There's another use for sums-over-histories. Hawking uses them to study all the different histories the universe could have and which are more probable than others.

As we continue, you'll need to know that even though the theory of relativity taught us to think of three dimensions of space and one of time as four dimensions of spacetime, there are still physical differences between space and time. One of these differences has to do with the way we measure the four-dimensional distance between two points in spacetime: the hypotenuse of the triangle you learned about earlier.

Figure 7-7a shows two separate events (*X* and *Y*) on a spacetime diagram. They are connected by a world-line at more than a 45-degree angle from the time-line. No information can pass between these events without exceeding the speed of light. In a case like this, where the distance between two events is greater in space than it is in time, the square of the hypotenuse (side *C*) of our triangle is a *positive* number. In the language of physics

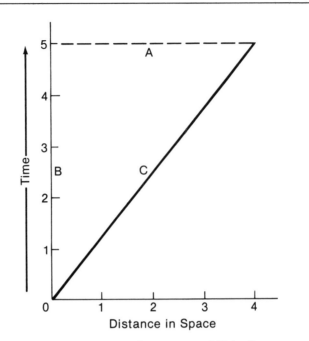

In our school geometry, the square of Side C (the hypotenuse) is equal to the sum of the squares of Sides A and B.

In the geometry of spacetime, the square of Side C (the hypotenuse) is equal to the DIFFERENCE between the squares of Sides A and B.

(Above) Figure 7-5. A right triangle, using the distance traveled in space as side A, the distance traveled in time as side B, and the world-line traveled in spacetime as side C, the hypotenuse.
(Right) Figure 7-6. The "twin paradox"

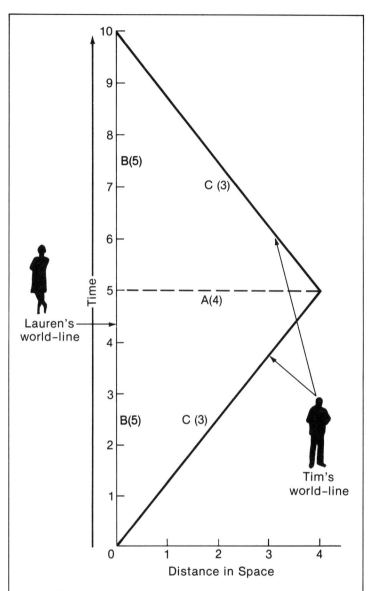

10

9

8

B(5)

7   C (3)

6

Time

5 - - - - - - - - - - - - - - - A(4)

Lauren's →
world-line

4

3

B(5)   C (3)

2

Tim's
world-line

1

0   1   2   3   4

Distance in Space

Tim travels 3 hours (by his watch) outward
bound and 3 hours homeward bound, at a
speed of four-fifths the speed of light. His
twin sister Lauren stays at home and doesn't
travel at all in space. While Lauren
measures ten hours on her watch, Tim only
measures six. He's four hours younger than
his twin sister when he returns to meet her.

the square of the "four-dimensional separation" between events X and Y is positive.

Figure 7-7b also shows two events. The distance between them is greater in time than it is in space. A world-line between these events runs at less than a 45-degree angle from the time-line. Information traveling at less than the speed of light can reach Y from X. When this is true, the square of the hypotenuse (side C) of our triangle is a *negative* number. Physicists say the square of the four-dimensional separation between X and Y is negative.

Perhaps you got lost in those last two paragraphs. If you didn't, a red light may have flashed on in your brain. The square of a number can't be negative. That doesn't happen in our math. If the square of a number were a negative number, what number could possibly be its square root? What is the square root, for instance, of -9? In our mathematics the square of any number (negative or positive) is always positive: 3 squared (3^2) is 9; so is -3 squared (-3^2). We can't possibly arrive at -9. It's impossible for the square of *anything* to be a negative number.

Stephen Hawking and other mathematicians and physicists have a way around this problem: Imagine that there are numbers that do produce negative numbers when multiplied by themselves, and see what happens. Say that imaginary one, when multiplied by itself, gives minus one. Imaginary two, multiplied by itself, gives minus four. Calculate the sums-over-histories of the particles and sums-over-histories of the universe using imaginary numbers. Figure them in "imaginary" rather than "real" time. The time it takes to get from

Figure 7-7. A distinction between space and time

110

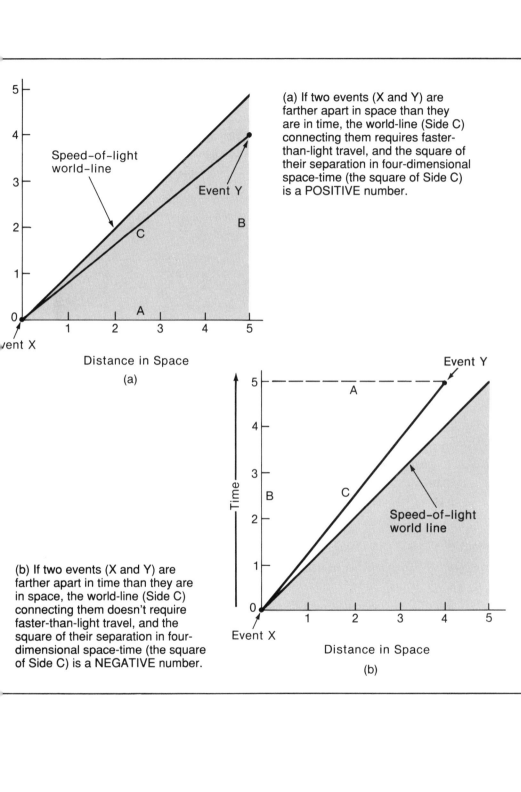

(a) If two events (X and Y) are farther apart in space than they are in time, the world-line (Side C) connecting them requires faster-than-light travel, and the square of their separation in four-dimensional space-time (the square of Side C) is a POSITIVE number.

Speed-of-light world-line

Event Y

C

B

A

0

Event X

Distance in Space

(a)

(b) If two events (X and Y) are farther apart in time than they are in space, the world-line (Side C) connecting them doesn't require faster-than-light travel, and the square of their separation in four-dimensional space-time (the square of Side C) is a NEGATIVE number.

Event Y

Time

A

B

C

Speed-of-light world line

Event X

Distance in Space

(b)

point X to point Y in Figure 7-7b is imaginary time—the square root of minus nine—imaginary three.

Imaginary numbers are a mathematical device (a trick, if you prefer) to help calculate answers that would otherwise be nonsense. "Imaginary time" allows physicists to study gravity on the quantum level in a better way, and it gives them a new way of looking at the early universe.

Smearing Out the Speed of Light?

Some of Hawking's colleagues are troubled by the following explanation, but Hawking assures us that in his opinion this is a correct way of thinking about it:

Traveling back into the very early universe, as space becomes more and more compressed, there are fewer possible choices about where a particle is (its position) at a given moment. The position becomes a more and more precise measurement. Because of the uncertainty principle this causes the measurement of the particle's velocity to become less and less precise.

First, let's look at the photon, the particle of light, under more normal circumstances. I've told you that photons move at 186,000 miles (300,000 kilometers) per second, making the speed of light 186,000 miles (300,000 kilometers) per second. Now I have to tell you that this might not always be the case. (Having read this far, you are accustomed to such reversals!) Photons, like electrons, can't simultaneously be pinned down precisely as to both position and velocity, because of the uncertainty principle. You learned that the probability of finding an electron is spread out over some region around the nucleus of an atom: more likely at some distances than others, but definitely a very smeary affair.

Just so, Richard Feynman and others have told us that the probability that a photon is traveling at 186,000 miles (300,000 kilometers) per second may be spread out over some "region" around that speed. That's the same as saying that in one way of thinking about it, the speed of a photon fluctuates more or less around what we call light speed. Over long distances probabilities cancel out, so as to make the speed of a photon 186,000 miles (300,000 kilometers) per second. However, over very small distances, on the quantum level, there's a possibility that a photon may move at slightly less or slightly more than this speed. These fluctuations won't be seen directly, but the path of photons on the space-time diagram, which we've drawn as a 45-degree angle, gets a little fuzzy.

When we're studying the very early universe, when space is very compressed, that line gets *very* fuzzy. The uncertainty principle means that the more precisely we measure the position of a photon, the less precisely we're able to measure its velocity. When we say that in the very early universe everything was packed to near-infinite density (not a singularity, but nearly there), we're becoming extraordinarily precise about the location of particles such as photons. When we are that precise about position, our imprecision about velocity vastly increases. As we near infinite density we also get near an infinite number of possibilities of what the speed of a photon is. What happens to our spacetime diagram now? Look at Figure 7-8. The world-line of a photon that in more normal circumstances is shown as a 45-degree angle becomes *terribly* smeared out. It fluctuates and ripples wildly.

Here is another way of thinking about what causes this "rippling," a way which will link it more clearly with other concepts you're reading about in this book: Traveling back into the very early universe is like shrinking ourselves to a size so unimaginably tiny that we can see what's happening on the level of the extremely small. Imagine it like this: If you look at this page, it seems smooth. You can curl the paper a bit, but

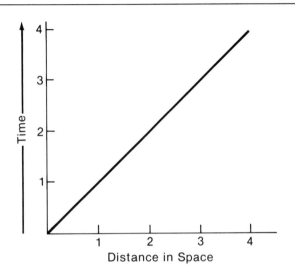

Normally a space-time diagram shows
the world-line of a photon, which travels
at light-speed, as a 45 degree angle.

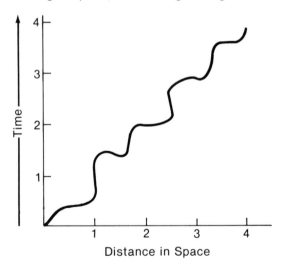

In the very early universe, when space is very
compressed, the smearing effect of the
uncertainty principle causes the world-line of a
photon to fluctuate wildly. We lose the basic
distinction between space and time.

it's still smooth. In the same way, although there is some curvature, spacetime around us seems smooth. On the other hand, if you look at this page under a microscope, you see curves and bumps. Similarly, if you look at spacetime on the extremely tiny level, billions on billions of times smaller than an atom, you find violent fluctuations in the geometry of spacetime (Figure 7-9). We'll discuss this again in Chapter 9 and learn that it might result in something called "wormholes." But for the time being the point is that we would find the same violent fluctuations in the very early universe, where everything was compressed to just such extreme smallness.

How can we explain this violent, chaotic scene? Again we turn to the uncertainty principle. We saw in Chapter 6 that the uncertainty principle also means that a field, such as an electromagnetic field or a gravitational field, can't have a definite value and a definite rate of change over time. Zero would be a definite measurement, so a field can't measure zero. All fields would *have* to measure exactly zero in empty space. So, no zero, no empty space. What do we have instead of empty space? A continuous fluctuation in the value of all fields, a wobbling a bit toward the positive and negative sides of zero so as to average out to zero but not *be* zero. This fluctuation can be thought of as the pairs of particles you learned about in the discussion of Hawking radiation. Particle pair production is greatest where the curvature of spacetime is most severe and changing most quickly. That's why we expect to find so many of them at the event horizon of a black hole.

*Figure 7-8. The uncertainty
principle in the early universe*

115

In the very early universe we find a situation of extremely great spacetime curvature and rapid change in that curvature. The quantum fluctuations in all fields, including the gravitational field, become very violent. If there are violent fluctuations in a gravitational field, that's the same as saying there are violent fluctuations in the curvature of spacetime. We're not talking about big curves, such as swells on the ocean. We're talking about all sorts of continuously changing crinkles and ripples and swirls. Odd things happen to the world-line of a photon in such a wild and weird environment. Again see Figures 7-8 and 7-9.

Whichever of these explanations we prefer, the point is that the difference between the time direction and directions in space disappears. When time looks like space, we no longer have our familiar situation in which the time direction always lies within the 45-degree angle and space directions always lie outside it.

Hawking sums up what we have just seen: "In the very early universe, when space was very compressed, the smearing effect of the uncertainty principle can

Figure 7-9. The quantum vacuum, as imagined by John Wheeler in 1957, becomes more and more chaotic as you inspect smaller regions of space. At the scale of the atomic nucleus (top), space still looks very smooth. Looking much more closely than that (middle), we see a roughness begin to appear. At a scale 1000 times smaller still (bottom), the curvature undergoes violent fluctuations.

116

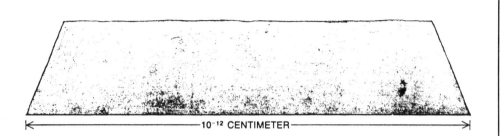

|←————————— 10^{-12} CENTIMETER ——————————→|

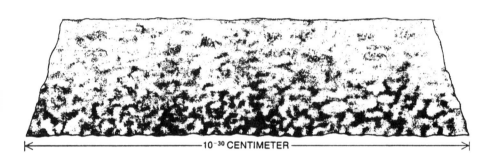

|←————————— 10^{-30} CENTIMETER ——————————→|

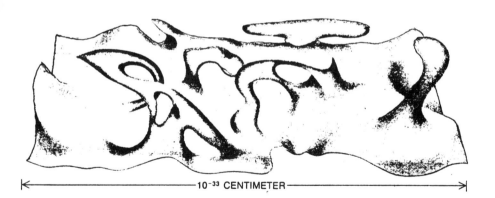

|←————————— 10^{-33} CENTIMETER ——————————→|

change the basic distinction between space and time." It's no longer true that if points are farther apart in time than they are in space, then the square of their separation in four-dimensional spacetime (the square of the hypotenuse of our triangle) is necessarily a negative number. "It is possible for the square of [that] separation to become positive under some circumstances. When this is the case, space and time lose their remaining distinction—we might say that time becomes fully spatialised—and it is then more accurate to talk, not of spacetime, but of a four-dimensional space."[4]

When Time Gets Spaced Out

What would this look like? How is this odd situation of four-dimensional space going to join smoothly with spacetime as we know it, in which time flows as time? Using imaginary time it's possible to picture four-dimensional space, where time as we know it is nonexistent, curving around and forming a closed surface, a surface without any edge or boundary. If you think you can picture this occurring in four dimensions, either you're mistaken or else you've taken a fresh evolutionary step in brain development. Most of us are doomed to think about it in fewer dimensions. It's easy to picture something with fewer dimensions that hasn't any edge or boundary: the surface of a ball or the surface of the earth.

We already mentioned that in the first Friedmann model of the universe, the universe was finite, not infinite, in size. But in that model it was also unbounded. It had no boundaries, no edges in space. It was like the surface of a ball: no edge, but not infinite in size. Hawking thinks the universe may be finite and unbounded in space *and time*. Time may have no beginning or end. All of it comes around and forms a closed surface, like the surface of the earth.

118

This leaves us fairly helpless. We can picture the surface of the earth, and we can agree that it is finite and unbounded, but what would a *universe* that is finite and unbounded in space and time be like? It's hard to make a mental connection between the shape of a ball and any meaningful concept of a four-dimensional universe. Just trying makes us feel quite blind—groping in the dark. Let's see what else we can say about it that might be helpful.

First, we'll say what it would *not* be like. There would be no "boundary conditions"—the way things were at the exact point of beginning—because there would be no point of beginning, no boundary, there: the whole thing would just curl around. Hawking suggests we state it exactly like that: the boundary conditions of the universe are that there are no boundaries. There would be no beginning and no end of the universe—*anywhere.* So don't even think of asking, But what about *before* that? That's like asking what's north of the North Pole. A signpost pointing "north" has no meaning at the North Pole. An arrow of time indicating "this way to the past" has no meaning when the time dimension has become "spacey."

Some of you are wondering, if there are no before and after the universe in the time dimension, would there be any "elsewhere," any other place, any outside of such a universe—in space dimensions? Hawking's model doesn't say that there isn't. Can you have an outside when you don't have any boundary? In the ball model there is a sense in which we do. It's in the direction the bug on the surface of the balloon in Chapter 4 would see if it could look "out" from the surface—which, you'll remember, it can't do. That dimension doesn't exist for the bug, but that doesn't necessarily mean it doesn't exist at all. The idea of having "elsewheres" in space but none in time (no before or after) fits nicely with the idea that the time we live in is only

119

a temporary mutation of what is really a fourth space dimension.

Since all of this may seem too complicated to be meaningful, let's look at it in another, more practical, way. Ask again, What would a universe that is finite and unbounded in space and time be like? The calculations are extremely difficult, and so far they've been carried out only in simple models. However, what they appear to be telling us is that a universe like that would be like our own.

As Hawking describes it: "They predict that the universe must have started out in a fairly smooth and uniform state. It would have undergone a period of what is called exponential or 'inflationary' expansion, during which its size would have increased by a very large factor but the density would have remained the same." Physicists who study the early universe believe our universe must have gone through just such an "inflationary" period. Hawking continues: "The universe would then have become very hot and would have expanded to the state that we see it today, cooling as it expanded. It would be uniform and the same in every direction on very large scales but would contain local irregularities that would develop into stars and galaxies."[5] In real time—and that's where we live—it would still appear to us that we have singularities at the beginning of the universe and inside black holes.

Hawking and a colleague, Jim Hartle of the University of California, Santa Barbara, presented the physics community with this no-boundary model of the universe in 1983. Hawking likes to emphasize that it is just a proposal. He hasn't deduced these boundary conditions from some other principle. The model appeals to him. He thinks "that it really underlies science because it is really the statement that the laws of science hold everywhere."[6] There are no singularities at which they break down. This kind of universe is self-contained. Do we have to explain how it was created? Would it have to be created at all? "It would just BE," writes Hawking.[7]

"What Place, Then, for a Creator?"

This raises some sticky philosophical questions. As Hawking puts it, "If the universe has no boundaries but is self-contained . . . then God would not have had any freedom to choose how the universe began."[8]

Hawking hasn't said that the no-boundary proposal rules out the existence of God, only that God wouldn't have had any choice in how the universe began. Other scientists disagree. They don't think the no-boundary proposal limits God very much. If God had no choice, we still have to wonder who decided that God would have no choice. Perhaps, suggests the physicist Karel Kuchar, *that* was the choice God made. Don Page, who reviewed *A Brief History of Time* for *Nature* magazine in England, has a similar viewpoint. Page lived with the Hawkings in the late 1970s when he was a postdoctoral researcher. He's now a professor at the University of Alberta, Canada, and still a good friend of Hawking's. They've collaborated on several scientific papers. To the question, What place, then, for a Creator? Page answers that in the Judeo-Christian view, "God creates and sustains the entire Universe rather than just the beginning. Whether or not the Universe has a beginning has no relevance to the question of its creation, just as whether an artist's line has a beginning and an end, or instead forms a circle with no end, has no relevance to the question of its being drawn."[9] A God existing outside our universe and our time wouldn't need a "beginning" in order to create, but it could still look to us, from our vantage point in "real" time, as though there had been a "beginning."

In *A Brief History of Time* Hawking himself suggests that there may still be a role for a Creator: "Is the unified theory so compelling that it brings about its own existence?" If not, "What is it that breathes fire into the equations and makes a universe for them to describe?"[10]

Which brings us to a word of caution: Although theoretical physicists ask challenging, penetrating questions and present us with mind-blowing proposals and theories, they do not give us ultimate answers. The best science progresses by suggesting "answers" and then taking apart and disproving those "answers." The most daring and imaginative scientists launch their toy boats and then try extremely hard to make them sink.

Hawking's work is a prime example. First he proved that the universe had to start as a singularity. Then with his no-boundary proposal he showed us how there might be no singularity after all. In the meantime he told us that black holes could never get smaller, and then he discovered they could. His work on the Big Bang singularity seemed consistent with a biblical view of Creation, but his no-boundary proposal put the Creator out of a job or at least changed the job description. In *A Brief History of Time* he suggests that we might need the Creator after all, and "the ultimate triumph of human reason" would be to "know the mind of God."[11] Hawking is provocative and open-minded in the way that the greatest thinkers have always been. He reaches clearly defined, well-supported conclusions, and then in the next breath he mercilessly questions and breaks down those same conclusions. He doesn't hesitate to admit that an earlier conclusion was incorrect or incomplete. That's the way his science—and perhaps all good science—advances, and one of the reasons why physics seems so full of paradoxes.

In the process Hawking, like the writers of the Bible and Shakespeare, has supplied eloquent quotations to support opposing philosophical points of view. He's been quoted and misquoted by those who believe in God and those who do not. He's been the hero and villain of both camps. However, those who depend on his statements—or statements of other scientists—to support their belief or unbelief risk having the rug swept out from under them at any moment.

Meanwhile, although it may appear to us that Hawking completely reversed himself with the no-boundary proposal, he doesn't see it that way. He says that the most important thing about his work on singularities was that it showed that a gravitational field must become so strong that you can't ignore quantum effects. And when you stop ignoring quantum effects, you find out that the universe could be finite in imaginary time but have no boundaries or singularities.

8

"It's turtles all the way down."

1983–1989

In the 1960s a practical need for a job, so that he could get married, sent Stephen Hawking off searching for singularities. In the 1980s another practical need—for funds to pay his daughter Lucy's school fees—launched him into a new enterprise that was to have a far-reaching impact on the Hawkings and others all over the world.

In the spring of 1982 Lucy was eleven years old and completing her final year at Newnham Croft School, a neighborhood grade school that cost nothing to attend. The best choice for the next stage of her education seemed to be a girls' school in Cambridge, the Perse School. Her brother Robert had been attending the Perse School for Boys since he was seven. Stephen Hawking decided to earn the money to pay Lucy's school fees by writing a book about the universe directed to people without a scientific education.

There had, of course, been other popular books

about the universe and black holes. However, Hawking thought none of them spoke enough about the most interesting questions, the questions that had made him want to study cosmology and quantum theory: Where did the universe come from? How and why did it begin? Will it come to an end and, if so, how? Is there a complete theory of the universe and everything in it? Are we close to finding that theory? Is there a need for a Creator?

These were questions that he thought should interest everybody, not only scientists. However, science had become so technical and specialized that the general public was left out of the discussion. The trick in writing the book would be to make it understandable to nonscientists, and that meant using virtually no mathematics. Hawking's editor warned him that every equation he used would cut book sales in half. Hawking considered that and eventually decided he would include only one equation: Einstein's $E = mc^2$.

Since it was going to be a great deal of trouble dictating a book of this length, Hawking thought it would be very good for the book to reach as many people as possible. His earlier books had been published by Cambridge University Press, a prestigious academic publisher. This time he wanted a publisher geared to the mass market. He wanted to see his book in airport bookstalls. His American agent discouraged this hope. Academics and students would buy the book, but the popular market, not likely.

Hawking completed the first draft in 1984. Against the advice of his agent, from among several offers he chose Bantam as the publisher. Bantam might never before have published a science book, but they sold many books in airports.

Hawking's editor at Bantam, who wasn't a scientist, felt that whatever he couldn't understand in the manuscript needed rewriting. He pointed out something that Hawking's students and colleagues had sometimes complained about: Because of the need to use few words, Hawking often jumped from thought to thought, wrongly assuming others could see the connection. What Hawking felt he'd explained simply was often unfathomable to others. Bantam tactfully suggested having an experienced science writer write the book for Hawking. Hawking vehemently rejected that idea.

The revision process was tedious. Each time Hawking submitted a rewritten chapter, his editor sent back a lengthy list of objections and questions. Hawking was irritated, but in the end he admits that the editor was right. "It is a much better book as a result," he says.[1]

While this revision process was going on, Hawking made a trip to Switzerland. Jane Hawking received an urgent summons to a hospital in Geneva. He had contracted pneumonia. She arrived to find him near death on a life-support system.

Hawking was choking, and doctors gave Jane Hawking the choice whether to allow an operation which would remove his windpipe. It might save his life, but afterward he'd never again be able to speak or make any vocal sound. That seemed a ghastly price to pay. Hawking's speech was slow and difficult to understand, but it was still speech, and his only possible means of communication. Without it he couldn't continue his career or even converse. What would survival be worth to him? With grave misgivings she ordered them to operate, then tried to set herself once more to give him the will to live.

"The future looked very, very bleak," she remembers. "We didn't know how we were going to be able to survive—or if he was going to survive. It was my decision . . . but I have sometimes thought—what have I done? What sort of life have I let him in for?"[2] Recov-

126

ering slowly in the hospital, Hawking no longer breathed through his mouth and nose, but through a small permanent opening made in his throat at about the height of his shirt collar. The only way he could communicate was to spell out words letter by letter by raising his eyebrows when someone pointed to the right letter on a spelling card.

After many weeks in intensive care Hawking went home. Jane Hawking was determined that he would stay with her and their children rather than live in a nursing home. Since 1980, community and private nurses had been coming for an hour or two each morning and evening to supplement the care given by Jane Hawking and the resident research student. However, from now on for as long as he lived, Hawking would need round-the-clock nurses. The cost was astronomical, far beyond the Hawkings' resources. The National Health Service, which in Britain is paid for by taxes, would have paid for a nursing home but could only offer a few hours' nursing care in the Hawkings' home plus help with bathing. "There was absolutely no way we could finance nursing at home,"[3] Jane Hawking says. Not only Hawking's work as a physicist but his life as a husband and father seemed at an end. It was an end they'd expected to come much sooner, but it was no less bitter for all that.

"At times things have looked absolutely dire for us and then something has come out of those crises,"[4] Jane has said with typical optimism. She turned to America for help. An American foundation offered fifty thousand pounds a year to pay for nurses. A computer expert in California, Walt Woltosz, sent a computer program he'd written, called Equalizer, which allows the user to select words from the computer screen. Hawking could operate it by a tiny movement that was still possible for him: squeezing a switch held in his hand. Should that fail him, head or eye movement could activate the switch.

Still too weak and ill to work on research, Hawking practiced with his computer. Before long he could produce ten words a minute, not very fast but good enough to convince him that he could continue his career. "It was a bit slow," he says, "but then I think slowly, so it suited me quite well." Since then, his speed has improved. He now produces more than fifteen words a minute.

The vocabulary programmed into the computer contains a few more than twenty-five hundred words. About two hundred of them are specialized scientific terms. Lines of words scroll by on the screen, highlighted one after the other. When the line he wants is highlighted, Hawking squeezes the switch. The words on that line are then highlighted one by one. When the word he wants is highlighted, he presses the switch again. Sometimes he misses, and the words or lines have to start over. There are also a few often-used phrases, such as "Please turn the page," "Please switch on the desk computer," and an alphabet for spelling out words not included in the program.

Hawking selects the words one by one to make a sentence, which appears across the lower part of the screen. He can send the result to a speech synthesizer, which pronounces it out loud or over the telephone, or he can save something on a disk and later print it out or rework it. He has a formatting program for writing papers, and he writes out his equations in words, which the program translates into symbols.

Hawking writes his lectures this way and saves them on disks. He can listen ahead of time to the speech synthesizer deliver a lecture, then edit and polish it. Before an audience he sends his lecture to the speech synthesizer a sentence at a time. An assistant shows slides, writes Hawking's equations on the board, and answers some of the questions.

Hawking's synthesized computer voice varies the intonation and doesn't sound like a robot, which to him is an extremely important feature. He wishes it gave him a British accent. Just what accent it does give him is uncertain. Some people say it's American or Scandinavian. To me it sounds East Indian. Hawking can't inject emotion into the voice. The effect is measured, thoughtful, and emotionally detached. Hawking's son Timmy thinks his father's voice suits him. Timmy of all the children is least able to remember what Hawking's own voice sounded like. When he was born in 1979, there was little of that left.

At first Hawking ran the Equalizer program only on his desktop computer. Later a friend, David Mason, adapted a small computer and speech synthesizer and attached it to the wheelchair, so that Hawking's voice goes with him wherever he goes.

Does all of this make conversation with Hawking seem like talking to a machine—like something alien, from science fiction? At first just a little. Soon you forget all about it. Hawking is comfortable with the odd situation and patient when others are not. When he was reading parts of this book while I held the pages, it was his nurse, not he, who suggested that it was unnecessary for me to wait for Hawking to select "Please turn the page," which involved a number of maneuvers on the computer screen. As soon as he started clicking, she said, I could turn the page and save him trouble and time. He'd put up with my way of doing things for an hour and a half without indicating that I was in any way inconveniencing him. As it happened, the next time Hawking "clicked" and I turned the page, he was making a comment, not asking for a page turn.

Hawking's sense of humor is contagious and likely

to break out at any time. When his haggard face lights up with a smile, it's difficult to believe this man has many problems. The Hawking grin is famous, and it reveals the quality of his love for his subject. It's a grin that says "This is all very impressive and serious, but— ain't it fun!"

It is, of course, nothing short of miraculous that Hawking has been able to achieve everything he has, even that he's still alive. However, when you meet him, and experience his intelligence and humor, you begin to take his unusual mode of communication and his obviously catastrophic physical problems no more seriously than he seems to himself. That is exactly the way he wants it. He chooses to ignore the difficulty, "not think about my condition, or regret the things it prevents me from doing, which are not that many."[5] He expects others to adopt the same attitude.

After the operation, when Hawking had recovered some of his strength and begun to master the computer program, he went to work again on his book and almost completely rewrote his first draft. He began to regard the new level of disability as an advantage rather than a calamity. "In fact," says Hawking, "I can communicate better now than before I lost my voice."[6] That statement is often quoted as an example of raw courage. It is, in fact, the simple truth. He no longer needs to dictate or speak through an "interpreter."

Hawking knew that even without equations, in nontechnical language, the concepts in his book wouldn't be easy for most people. He claims he's not overly fond of equations himself, in spite of the fact that people compare his ability to handle them in his head with Mozart's mentally composing a whole symphony. It's not easy for him to write equations, and he says he has no intuitive feeling for them. He likes to think instead in pictures, and this seemed an excellent method for the book: to describe his mental images in words, helped along with familiar analogies and a few diagrams.

He wondered just how much to explain. Were some complicated matters better glossed over and left at that? Would explaining too much lead to confusion? Ultimately Hawking explained a great deal. Perhaps thanks to his persistent editor, he made it possible (though not always easy) to follow him logically from thought to thought, sometimes even to anticipate him. This is a book to be studied, if you don't have a scientific background, not read quickly. It's well worth the effort, and it's also good entertainment. Hawking's humor makes *A Brief History of Time* in its way a romp through the history of time, not safe to read in any situation where it would be awkward to burst out laughing.

When the book was nearing publication, Hawking's editor left Bantam to take another job. New editors at Bantam got nervous about this strange scientific book and ordered a small first printing. That had to be recalled because it was full of errors: photographs and diagrams in the wrong places and wrongly labeled. Not a promising beginning, but, like so many Hawking disasters in the past, it turned into a bit of luck.

Before the book was reissued, *Time* magazine featured an article about Hawking. Bantam revised their estimation of him and, feeling a little more optimistic, ordered a larger printing. However, no one predicted the phenomenal success the book was to have.

The Hawkings watched *A Brief History of Time: From the Big Bang to Black Holes* climb effortlessly to the top of the best-seller lists. There it stayed week after unlikely week, then month after month, soon selling a million copies in America. In Britain the publisher could barely keep enough books on the shelves to meet the demand. Translations into other languages quickly followed. The book was indeed prominently displayed in airport bookstalls.

Stephen Hawking rapidly became a household word and a popular hero all over the world. Fans organized a club in Chicago and printed Hawking T-shirts. One member admitted that some of his school friends think this Hawking on his T-shirt must be a rock star; a few even claim to have his latest album.

Reviews of the book were favorable. One compared it to *Zen and the Art of Motorcycle Maintenance.* Jane Hawking was horrified, but Stephen Hawking declared he was flattered, that this means his book "gives people the feeling that they need not be cut off from the great intellectual and philosophical questions."[7]

Do people who buy the book read it and understand it? Hawking said he wasn't overly concerned about its being left on coffee tables and bookcases just for show. The Bible and Shakespeare, he pointed out, have shared that fate for centuries. Nevertheless, he thinks lots of people have read his book, because he gets mounds of letters about it. Many ask questions and make detailed comments. He's often stopped by strangers in the street who say how much they enjoyed it; this pleases him immensely but embarrasses his son Timmy.

Hawking loves to travel. His increasing celebrity status and the need to publicize the book gave him plenty of opportunities. A Hawking visit usually leaves his hosts exhausted. The Rockefeller Institute in New York was the scene of one such visit. After a long day of lectures and public appearances there was a banquet in Hawking's honor. Although he no longer has any sense of taste or smell, Hawking relishes such occasions and makes a show of sniffing the wine and commenting on it. Dinner and speeches over, the party moved to the embankment overlooking the East River. Everyone was petrified lest Hawking roll into the river. To their relief he didn't, and they soon had him safely headed back toward his hotel. In a ballroom opening off the lobby, a dance was going on. Hawking insisted that they not go to bed yet but crash the party. Unable to dissuade their headstrong honoree, the little group of distinguished scholars hesitatingly agreed, "although we never do anything like that!" On the dance floor Hawking twirled about in his wheelchair with one partner after another. The band went on playing for him far into the night, long after the original party was over.

Will Hawking write a sequel to his book? He thinks not. "What would I call it? *A Longer History of Time? Beyond the End of Time? Son of Time?*"[8] Perhaps *A Brief History of Time II*—"just when you thought it was safe to go back into the airport bookstore!" Will he write his autobiography? Not until he runs out of money to pay his nurses, or so he told me. That's not likely to be soon. *Time* magazine announced in August 1990 that *A Brief History of Time* had so far sold over 8 million copies.

Some accuse Bantam and Hawking of exploiting Hawking's condition in marketing the book. They say his fame and popularity are like a carnival sideshow, and they blame Hawking for allowing an overdramatic, grotesque picture to appear on the cover. Hawking claims his contract gave him absolutely no control over the cover. He did persuade the publisher to use a better picture on the British edition.

On the plus side, the media exposure has allowed Hawking to give us something that may be even more valuable than his scientific theories and the information that the universe is probably not "turtles all the way down." It has brought to millions all over the world not only his keen excitement about his work but also the important truth that there is health which transcends the boundaries of any illness.

For the Hawkings the success of the book brought

more than a change in financial status. For years they had lived with disability and the threat of death. As Jane Hawking describes it, "In a sense we've always been living on the edge of the precipice, and eventually you put down roots at the edge of the precipice. I think that's what we've done."[9] Now they found themselves threatened in a different way, by the allure and demands of celebrity and the frightening prospect of living up to a worldwide fairy-tale image.

"The field of baby universes is in its infancy but growing fast."

1988–1990

As early as the 1970s, magazine articles and television specials had told Stephen Hawking's story. In the late 1980s, after publication of *A Brief History of Time*, virtually every periodical in the world profiled him. Reporters and photographers greeted him everywhere. "COURAGEOUS PHYSICIST KNOWS THE MIND OF GOD," blared the headlines. His picture was on the cover of *Newsweek* with the words "MASTER OF THE UNIVERSE" emblazoned across a dramatic background of stars and nebulae. In 1989 he and his family were interviewed for ABC's show "20/20," and in England a new television special appeared: "Master of the Universe: Stephen Hawking." Hawking was no longer merely well known and successful. He'd become an idol, a superstar, in a class with sports heroes and rock musicians. Meanwhile, the academic awards kept pouring in: five more honorary degrees and seven more international awards.

Jane Hawking spoke of her "sense of fulfillment that we have been able to remain a united family, that the children are absolutely superb and that Stephen is still able to live at home and do his work."[1] By this time Robert Hawking was a university student at Cambridge, studying physics and rowing for his college, Corpus Christi. One of the television specials showed him racing on the river while the rest of the family, including Hawking with his synthetic voice, cheered from the bank. Lucy was eighteen and considering a career in the theater. She would take a year off and then go to Oxford. As for ten-year-old Tim, Hawking said, "Of all my children, he is probably the one most like me."[2] He and Tim enjoyed playing games. Hawking usually won at chess, Tim at Monopoly. "So we're both quite good at something," proclaimed Tim.[3] In 1988 the American photographer Stephen Shames took pictures of them engaged in an impromptu game of hide-and-go-seek. Tim excelled at that. He could tell when his father was getting near by the hum of the wheelchair motor.

Lucy told interviewers that she and her father "get on quite well," though both are stubborn. "I've had lots of arguments with him actually, I must admit, with neither of us willing to give ground. I think a lot of people don't realize just how stubborn he is. Once he gets an idea in his head, he will follow it through no matter what the consequences are. He doesn't let a thing drop." "He will do what he wants to do at any cost to anybody else."[4] This sounds harsh, but when you speak with Lucy, it's quite clear she's enormously fond of her father and respects his opinions. She went on in the interview to say that she thinks he *has* to be stubborn in his situation. It's a necessary mode of survival for him. His strength of will keeps him working day in day out, grinning and delivering funny one-liners and ignoring a grim physical situation. If it also occasionally makes him appear spoiled and self-centered, it seems entirely reasonable to forgive him. About his health and the fear of his dying, Lucy says, "I always think 'Oh he's going to

be all right,' because he's always pulled through everything that's happened to him. You can't help worrying
about someone who's so frail. I get quite worried when
he goes away."[5]

In the academic world physicists continued to express tremendous respect for Hawking but were a little
nonplussed by all the media hype. It didn't take higher
math to multiply book sales figures in the millions and
find they amount to more than Lucy's school fees. There
was an occasional hint of sour grapes, a half-suppressed
mutter of "His work's no different from a lot of other
physicists; it's just that his condition makes him interesting." But there has been surprisingly little of that.
Hawking can more than hold his own in any company,
and everybody knows it. Moreover, his colleagues enjoy
him. Sidney Coleman of Harvard, who rivals Hawking
not only as a physicist but also as a classroom come-
dian, is pleased that Hawking's celebrity brings him
more and more often to America, and frequently to New
England. Other physicists who are sometimes unfairly
eclipsed by Hawking nevertheless don't blame him personally.

However, it isn't unreasonable to suggest that
Hawking's scientific accomplishments alone would
never have made him the celebrity he is or sold millions
of books. Are those correct who say he's exploited his
pathetic condition and ridden his wheelchair to fame
and fortune? The truth is, although Hawking would almost certainly prefer it otherwise, most of the world
probably appreciates him more for his spirit than for
his scientific achievements. He's not the only person
who's overcome staggering odds and maintained a positive attitude in adverse circumstances, but who else
has done it with quite such brilliant success and engaging style?

For over a quarter century Stephen Hawking, perhaps with lapses we'll never know about, had kept up

this spirit of optimism and determination for his own benefit. His survival and success depended on his doing so. However, it was a responsibility only to himself and to his family. Now, in the late 1980s, it became a responsibility to millions all over the world for whom he was an inspiration. Many, not only the disabled, expected him to go on proving that, in spite of tragedy, life and people could still be absolutely splendid. We shouldn't be surprised if Hawking was leery about having that larger responsibility thrust on him. He was, he said, no more than simply human.

For disabled people Hawking had become a superb role model, but the disparity between what he'd achieved and what most can expect is sometimes discouraging. In everything except his illness Hawking has been outrageously lucky. Few will find a Jane Hawking. Few have Hawking's powers of concentration and self-control. Few have his genius.

Jane Hawking pointed out that if her husband were an obscure physics teacher, she couldn't have convinced a foundation to donate over fifty thousand pounds a year for nurses. There would be no computer program. He would be sitting day after pointless day in a nursing facility, away from his home and family, mute, isolated, and wasted. Her bitterness about the way the National Health Service (NHS) failed them led her to campaign for those with similar problems, trying to get the NHS to provide money for home nursing rather than tear apart families. The Hawking image has encouraged universities to set up dormitories equipped for students needing round-the-clock nurses in order to attend classes. An abstract glass minisculpture sits on a filing cabinet in Hawking's office, a gift from "Hawking House," a dormitory at the University of Bristol. Funds are being raised in Cambridge for a similar facility.

Whatever the effect on the rest of the world, in 1989 Stephen Hawking had "made it," against stupendous odds. The queen named him "Companion of Honor," one of the highest honors she can bestow. Cambridge University did what it rarely does and gave one of its own faculty an honorary doctorate. Hawking received his degree from Prince Philip, chancellor of the university, and joined in the pageantry, going to and from the Senate House to the accompaniment of the choirs of King's College and St. John's College and the Cambridge University Brass Ensemble. "This year has been the crowning glory of all Stephen's achievements," Jane Hawking said. "I think he is very happy about it."[6] He loved doing the work he did. "I have a beautiful family, I am successful in my work, and I have written a best-seller. One really can't ask for more," he said.[7] He'd earned this fame, and he was enjoying it. For someone who'd thought at age twenty-one that he had no reason to go on living, it was heady stuff indeed, a delicious joke on fate.

If there was a down side, it was easy to ignore. There was less time for his scientific work: Too many "extra-curricular activities," his students lamented. Too many visitors, but he loved to receive them and seldom turned anyone away. Too many invitations, but he seemed incapable of refusing them. He loved traveling and did more and more of it. Too much mail: it was impossible to answer every letter personally. His graduate assistant and his secretary took on major responsibility for answering his mail.

As Hawking juggled his increasingly unmanageable schedule, colleagues began to worry that he would neglect his science. However, Hawking's scientific work did continue. While he traveled the globe as a celebrity, in his head he traveled distances that make these journeys seem paltry by comparison. John Wheeler of Princeton had earlier (in 1956) introduced the idea of "quantum wormholes." Hawking now was adventuring through these wormholes into even more exotic climes:

"baby universes." Let's stand with him outside space and time, to get a better view.

A New Look at the Cosmic Balloon

Imagine an enormous balloon, inflating rapidly. The balloon represents our universe. Dots on the surface represent stars and galaxies. The dots cause dimples and puckers in the surface. As Einstein predicted, the presence of matter and/or energy causes a warping of space-time.

When we look at the cosmic balloon through a not-very-powerful microscope, the surface, regardless of the puckers, looks relatively smooth. Looking through a much more powerful microscope, we find it isn't smooth after all. The surface seems to be vibrating furiously, creating a blur, a fuzziness (see Figure 7-9).

We've seen such fuzziness before. In Chapter 2 and later chapters, you learned that the uncertainty principle causes the universe to be a very fuzzy affair at the quantum level. It's never possible to know precisely both the position and the velocity of a particle at the same time. One way to picture this quantum uncertainty is by imagining that each particle jitters in a sort of random microscopic vibration. The closer we try to look, the more violently it jitters. Scrutinize the quantum level with the greatest possible care, and we at best are able to say only that a particle has *this* probability of being *here*—or *that* probability of moving like *that*.

The surface of the cosmic balloon is unpredictable in a similar way. Under high enough magnification the quantum fluctuation becomes so incredibly chaotic that we can say there's a probability for it to be doing—*anything.*

What does Stephen Hawking think this "anything" might be? He thinks there's a probability that the cosmic balloon will develop a little bulge in it. More famil-

140

iar balloons, the ones at parties, do that if one point on the surface is weak. Usually party balloons burst immediately when that happens, but on rare occasions a miniature balloon bulges out of the surface. If you could see this happening to our cosmic balloon, you would be witnessing the birth of a "baby universe."

It sounds spectacular: the birth of a universe. Will we ever witness such an event? No, first because it happens in imaginary time, which you read about in Chapter 7, not "real" time. Another reason we won't see it, says Hawking, is that if anything can truly be said to start small, it's a universe. The most probable size for the connection between our universe and the new baby—the umbilical cord, if you will—is only about 10^{-33} centimeters across. To write that fraction you use 1 as the numerator and 1 followed by thirty-three zeros for the denominator. That's small! The opening—the **wormhole**, as it's called—is like a tiny black hole, flickering into existence and then vanishing after an interval too short to imagine. We've spoken of something else with an extremely short life span: In Chapter 5, when we discussed Hawking radiation, you learned that you can think of fluctuations in an energy field as pairs of very short-lived particles. Wormholes similarly are a way of thinking about fluctuations in the fabric of spacetime: the surface of the cosmic balloon.

The baby universe attached to this umbilical cord may *not* be short-lived, and small beginnings don't always continue small. Eventually the new universe might expand to become something like our present universe, extending billions of light-years.

Like our universe, but empty? Not at all. "Matter," Hawking points out, "can be created in any size universe out of gravitational energy."[8] The result might later be galaxies, stars, planets, and, perhaps, life.

Are there many baby and grown-up universes? Do they branch off everywhere? Right here inside your

141

room? Inside your body? Yes, it may be that new universes are constantly coming into existence all around us, even from points inside us, completely undetectable to our senses.

Perhaps you're wondering whether our universe began as a bulge from the side of another. It's possible, declares Hawking. Our universe may be part of an infinite labyrinth of universes, branching off and joining one another like a never-ending honeycomb, involving not only a lot of baby universes but adult universes as well. Two universes could develop wormhole connections in more than one spot. Wormholes might link parts of our own universe with other parts of it, or with other times (Figure 9-1).

Life in the Quantum Sieve

Let's stretch our imaginations and look at all of this from the point of view of an electron. If there are quadrillions of wormholes flickering in and out of existence at every point in the universe, an electron is facing something like an enormous, furiously boiling pot of thick porridge. Moving across it is about as tricky as traveling across a giant, continuously changing sieve. An electron trying to move in a straight line in such an environment is almost certain to encounter a wormhole, fall in, and go shooting off into another universe. That sounds suspiciously as though matter will be disappearing from our universe, which you'll remember isn't allowed. However, that isn't happening. An identical electron comes back the other way and pops into our universe.

Figure 9-1. Wormholes
and baby universes

142

A wormhole leading from
our universe to another

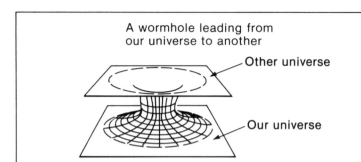

Other universe

Our universe

A wormhole connecting one part of
our universe with another part

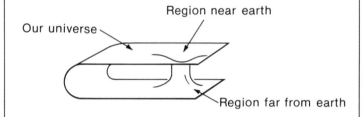

Region near earth

Our universe

Region far from earth

Part of a labyrinth of
interconnecting universes

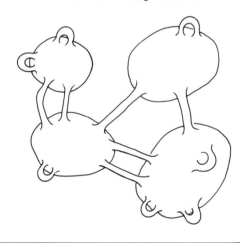

Wouldn't we notice this substitution of electrons? We won't see it that way. To us this event will look like one electron moving in a straight line. The presence of wormholes, however, will make all electrons move as though they have a higher mass than they would if there were no wormholes. Therefore, if we're to try to predict particle masses with any theory, it's important to know whether or not there really are such things as wormholes.

The theory says that if an electron falls into a wormhole accompanied by a photon, it won't appear to be anything out of the ordinary. We will observe only the normal exchange of a messenger particle in an electromagnetic interaction, in which one electron emits a photon and another absorbs it. Hawking suggests that perhaps all particle masses and all particle interactions—the ceaseless activity of the four forces, all over the universe—can be explained as this going into and out of wormholes.

You would be right to wonder, at this point, how particles can possibly pass through wormholes. Wormholes are much smaller than even the smallest particles we know. As with Hawking radiation, what is impossible in any way we try to picture it *is* possible in quantum mechanics.

When Hawking calculated the effect of wormholes on the masses of particles such as electrons, his calculations at first suggested that the masses would be much larger than we actually observe for these particles. He and other researchers have since managed to come up with more reasonable numbers. However, at present Hawking doubts whether wormhole theory can predict the masses of particles for our universe or any other. As you learned in Chapter 2, when something must be measured directly and cannot be predicted by the theory, that's called an arbitrary element. The masses of particles and the strengths of the forces are, in every theory anyone has come up with so far, just such arbitrary elements.

Wormhole theory may not make them any less arbitrary, but it may explain how they happen to be arbitrary. Hawking thinks the masses of particles and other fundamental numbers in nature may turn out to be "quantum variables." That means they may be uncertain, like the paths of particles or what happens on the surface of the cosmic balloon. These numbers would be fixed at random at the moment of creation in each universe. A throw of the dice, so to speak, and then that's settled for that particular universe—but no way to know from a theory how the dice will fall, or perhaps even to say that one way is definitely more probable than another. This may or may not be the case in wormhole theory. The jury is still out.

The Problem of the Curling-Up Universe—Revisited

"It is a great mystery why quantum fluctuations do not warp spacetime into a tiny ball," says Hawking.[9] You'll recall that this is one of the enigmas that theorists must solve in the quest for the Theory of Everything.

Physicists refer to this problem of the energy in the (so-called) vacuum as the cosmological constant problem. You'll remember that Einstein theorized about something called the cosmological constant, which would balance gravity and prevent the universe from changing in size. He later called it "the greatest blunder of my life." The term has come to have a related but slightly different meaning. The *cosmological constant*, as scientists now use the term, is a number which tells us how densely this energy in the vacuum is packed: the energy density of the vacuum. Common sense says there shouldn't be any energy there at all, but, as you've learned, the uncertainty principle shows that "empty" space isn't empty. It seethes with energy. The cosmo-

145

logical constant (the energy density of the vacuum) ought to be enormous, and general relativity theory tells us this mass/energy should be curling up the universe.

However, regardless of what the uncertainty principle and theory of general relativity indicate, we don't have a curled-up universe. Quite the contrary, the value (the number) of the cosmological constant is observed to be near zero. We find this out by observing the rate at which galaxies are moving away from one another, and from the fact of our own existence. "A large cosmological constant either positive or negative would make the universe unsuitable for the development of life," Hawking points out.[10] The value of the cosmological constant is one of the examples of the "fine-tuning" we saw in Chapter 6.

How can the cosmological constant possibly be zero, as we observe, when theory tells us it should be enormous? Recall once again the particle pairs you learned about in Chapter 5, when we discussed Hawking radiation. Supergravity, the theory Hawking spoke of in his Lucasian lecture, tells us that pairs of fermions (matter particles) in the vacuum give negative energy and balance the positive energy of pairs of bosons (messengers). This may indeed be the explanation, or at least part of it, but it's a complicated matter. For one thing, these particles don't only interact with gravity. However, even if we do have a lot of positives and negatives canceling one another out, for all of these to cancel out to zero is a little too much to swallow. As Sidney Coleman, who shares Hawking's enthusiasm for wormholes, puts it, "Zero is a suspicious number. Imagine that over a ten-year period you spend millions of dollars without looking at your salary, and when you finally compare what you spent with what you earned, they balance out to the penny."[11] For the cosmological constant to balance out to zero is even less likely.

146

Can wormholes solve the mystery? Hawking believes that wormholes branching off at every point make the cosmological constant, the energy density of the vacuum, a "quantum variable" like the masses of particles. It can have *any* value. What's the probability of its being near zero?

Imagine the birth of a universe as a "baby" branching off from an existing universe. Wormhole theory says there are plenty of universes—some more enormous than ours is today, others unimaginably smaller than an atom, and all sizes in between. The infant universe must copy its cosmological constant value from one of these other universes through a wormhole—"inherit" it, you might say. It isn't important to a human infant whether it inherits a talent for music; it becomes important only when the infant grows larger. It isn't important to a baby universe whether it "inherits" a cosmological constant value near zero. Its cosmological constant value won't even be measurable until it's quite a bit more grown up. However, with all those assorted sizes of universes around, the infant is far more likely to inherit its cosmological constant value through wormhole attachments with large, cooler universes of the sort only possible when all those positives and negatives in the vacuum cancel out to zero. Coleman studied the probability of a universe (in wormhole theory) being a universe where the cosmological constant is near zero: our kind of universe. He found that any *other* sort of universe would be highly unlikely.

Wormholes and the Theory of Everything

Wormholes and baby universes are firing the imaginations of many physicists. They've begun responding, disputing this and that, and offering alternative versions. That's always a good sign. "The field of baby universes

147

is in its infancy," quips Hawking, "but growing fast."[12] Do wormholes and baby universes contribute to the search for a complete theory of the universe?

First of all, we've seen that the theory gives us a new way of looking at the problem of the cosmological constant, the sticky question of the energy density in the vacuum, which ought to be shrinking the universe but isn't. Does Hawking think wormholes are the theory that will solve this inconsistency between general relativity and quantum mechanics? "I would not go so far as that," Hawking says. "There is no fundamental inconsistency, but there are technical problems which wormholes don't help."[13]

Second, wormhole theory is a theory that doesn't break down if you follow it back to the "beginning." Remember that with Einstein's theories, if you follow things back to the Big Bang, you reach a singularity where the laws of physics as we know them break down. Hawking's no-boundary proposal showed that in imaginary time there would be no singularity. Wormhole theory suggests that in imaginary time our universe may have begun as a baby universe branching off from another universe.

Third, wormhole theory links quantum theory and relativity theory in a satisfying, geometric way. It allows us to think of quantum fluctuations, quantum wormholes, and baby universes as not too different from the warping of spacetime and black holes on the astronomical level. It tells us that the fundamental numbers in our universe, such as the masses and charges of particles and the cosmological constant, may be the result of the shape, the geometry, of a labyrinth of interconnected universes.

Other theories can't predict the masses and charges of particles. These are arbitrary elements in the theories. An alien who had never seen our universe couldn't take these theories and use them to calculate what these fundamental quantities are, without peeking at the "real" universe. We've seen that there is still much argument about whether wormholes may give us a way of understanding and calculating these fundamental numbers, or whether wormholes make their prediction less likely with any theory.

Theorists who work in the field of superstring theory, which says that the fundamental objects in the universe are not pointlike particles after all but tiny vibrating strings, hope their theory will eventually be able to predict particle masses and charges. Hawking is pessimistic. He says, "If this picture of baby universes is correct, our ability to predict these quantities will be reduced."[14] If we knew how many universes there are out there and what their sizes are, it would be different, but we don't know that. We can't even see their joining onto or branching off our own. We can't get an accurate picture of the shape of it all. We know only that if universes do join on or branch off, this changes the apparent values of such quantities as particle masses and charges. We end up with a small but definite amount of uncertainty in the predicted values.

Hawking meanwhile doesn't worry overly much about whether his work is leading him to the Theory of Everything. His strategy is to concentrate on areas he understands, chipping away at the problem of what happens and how things work when relativity and quantum mechanics are taken together. What he discovers about the universe in this way should hold true, he thinks, regardless of what the theory of everything turns out to be and who finds it. His picture should fit in as part of the larger, or more basic, picture.

"Think Imaginary"

Science fiction buffs will be disappointed if we don't discuss the possibility that something larger than a par-

149

ticle can travel through a wormhole into another universe or into another part of our universe. There's been a lot of speculation about the possibility of wormholes inside black holes. On the face of it this form of travel seems as though it ought to be possible. The problem is that a wormhole inside a black hole, one large enough for you or me to get through, would be dangerously unstable. Even so small a disturbance as our presence would destroy the wormhole, and us with it.

What about a smaller black hole? In Chapter 5 we learned about primordial black holes. When they evaporate, what happens to things that fell into them earlier? Wormhole theory suggests that they may not necessarily return to our universe as particles. The particles instead may slip off into a baby universe. This baby universe might join on again to our region of space-time. Then it would look like another black hole, which formed and evaporated. Things falling into one black hole would emerge as particles from the other black hole, and vice versa. That's space travel of a sort—if you happen to be a particle.

However, there's another snag to it. All of this happens in imaginary time: the time we encountered in Chapter 7, where time becomes like another space dimension. As Hawking describes it,

> In real time, an astronaut who fell into a black hole would come to a sticky end. He would be torn apart by the difference between the gravitational force on his head and his feet. Even the particles that made up his body would not survive. Their histories, in real time, would come to an end at a singularity. However, the histories of the particles in imaginary time would continue. They would pass into the baby universe, and would re-emerge as the particles emitted by another black hole. Thus, in a sense, the astronaut

150

would be transported to another region of the universe. However, the particles that emerged would not look much like the astronaut. Nor might it be much consolation to him, as he ran into the singularity in real time, to know that his particles will survive in imaginary time. The motto for anyone who falls into a black hole must be: Think Imaginary.[15]

10

"Is the end in sight for theoretical physics?"

1990–1991

Stephen Hawking's office at the Department of Applied Mathematics and Theoretical Physics in Cambridge isn't glamorous. The building is large and old but not beautiful. The entrance is off Silver Street, about a block away from Queens College and the Silver Street Bridge across the River Cam. You enter through an uninviting alleyway, an asphalt carpark, and a red door. Hawking enters through a rear door via his ramp.

The interior is institutional, the floor plan pieced together illogically. A corridor beyond the small reception area makes an abrupt right turn past a behemoth of a black metal elevator, continues straight for a while, then bends and widens past letterboxes and overstuffed bulletin boards with lecture and seminar notices and some lewd graffiti, narrows again abruptly, and ends at the door of a large common room.

In this common room the DAMTP gathers for tea every afternoon at 4:00, but for most of the day the room is deserted and dimly lighted. The color scheme shows a preference for lime green—in vinyl armchairs grouped around low tables, woodwork, and the lower halves of the pillars that hold up the high ceiling. There's a table with stacks of scientific publications, a rogues' gallery of small photos of present students and faculty on one wall, formal portraits of former Lucasian professors on another. At the far end of the room enormous windows provide a view of a blank wall across the alley and admit little light.

Hawking's office and a number of others open off this common room. On his door there's a small placard: "QUIET PLEASE, THE BOSS IS ASLEEP." Probably not true. Hawking has spent long hours working in that pleasant, high-ceilinged office with his computers, photos of his children, a few plants, a life-size picture of Marilyn Monroe on the door, and always one of his nurses in attendance. His one oversized window overlooks the carpark.

Hawking's day there begins at 11:00 A.M. His secretary, Sue Masey, reviews his schedule with him. That's become something of a joke. They seldom manage to follow it, and anyone who has an appointment with Hawking must remain flexible.

The day continues with the soft clicking of his hand-held pressure switch. Propped in his chair, Hawking watches the computer screen impassively and selects words to converse with visitors and interviewers, consult colleagues, advise students, converse over the telephone, write lectures, or answer correspondence. Sometimes you hear the soft hum of his wheelchair motor as he guides it by means of a joystick through the common room and corridors to other rooms in the building for meetings and seminars, always accompanied by a nurse. At intervals the well-modulated computer voice requests his nurse to adjust his position in the chair or suction fluid that accumulates in his breathing passage.

Hawking's nursing staff is large and competent and varied as to age and sex. They seem indulgently fond of

153

Hawking and devoted to the task of making him look nice, keeping his hair brushed, his glasses clean, his chin wiped of the saliva that runs from his mouth, and, as they put it, to "getting him sorted out" many times a day. Hawking has no choice but to be totally dependent on others, but there's no air of helplessness about him. He seems vigorous and decisive, unquestionably in charge of his life. The strength of his personality makes working for him and with him both rewarding and demanding.

At 1:00, rain or shine, Hawking propels his wheelchair with portable computer attached into the narrow Cambridge streets, sometimes accompanied only by a nurse, sometimes by students, who trot to keep up with him. It's a short journey through the heart of Cambridge, past the up-market shops in King's Parade, King's College Chapel, and the Senate House, to Gonville and Caius, to dine with other Fellows of his college. There a nurse arranges a bib around his shoulders and spoons food into his mouth.

After lunch there's the return journey. Hawking is notorious for his hair-raising wheelchair driving. Students bound ahead into traffic on King's Parade and Silver Street to stop cars, lorries, and bicycles as he recklessly barrels ahead assuming the right-of-way. Acquaintances fear he's more likely to be crushed by a truck than die from ALS.

At 4:00 Hawking usually emerges again from behind his lime green door. Teatime is a ritual in the department, and the empty, cavernous room becomes suddenly deafeningly noisy with voices and the clatter of teacups. Most of the assembled physicists and mathematicians dress as though they are on a construction site. Someone has commented that Hawking's "relativity group" looks like a rock group on a bad day. Their talk isn't small talk. It ranges among wormholes, Euclidean regions, scalar fields, and black holes. Equations are scrawled on the low table. "When we want to save something, we Xerox the table,"[1] says Hawking. His wry wit sets the tone in his corner of the room, but students claim that a few remarks from him during tea are often more valuable than an hour lecture by somebody else. Hawking has indeed mastered the art of packing a lot into a few words. Reading over notes later, you realize how precisely he's chosen his words to say exactly what he means.

At 4:30 the common room empties as rapidly as it filled, and all but one of the long, fluorescent lighting fixtures is switched off. Hawking glides back into his office to work until 7:00. In the late afternoon his students find him more available to help them.

On some evenings Hawking dines in college, or in a specially equipped van bought with award money from the Israeli Wolf Prize in physics, he's driven to a concert or the theater. When there's a concert at Tim's school, he goes to hear Tim play the cello with the orchestra. Tim is a fine cellist, following in the footsteps of his sister Lucy.

In 1990 the frenzy of celebrity was altering this picture slightly. Now it wasn't just another television personality interviewing Hawking for a special. It was a director from Stephen Spielberg's company whisking him off for the filming of *A Brief History of Time*. Hawking's office was re-created on the set so that one wall could seem to pan out into the universe. It wasn't just a local Cambridge or New York photographer, but Francis Giacobetti, photographer of the pope and Federico Fellini, whose equipment and assistants crowded the common room near Hawking's door. The mail had become an impossible burden for Hawking's research assistant, his secretary, and one of his nurses, who now helped them. They struggled valiantly to write thoughtful answers to letters, poems, videotapes from all over the world, many of which told moving stories and de-

155

served a personal response. They felt sad and guilty to have to resort increasingly to polite preprinted post-cards. It would have taken all Hawking's waking hours to handle even a fraction of his mail.

Life at the center of so much attention and adulation takes on an unnatural cast. It isn't easy to keep things in perspective, no matter how levelheaded and grown up you are or how good a sense of humor you have about yourself. For a quarter of a century Hawking had been convincing people that he was not subhuman. He'd succeeded too well. He'd convinced them he was superhuman. He'd never deliberately encouraged this idea. He'd said he refused to be treated as less *or more* than simply human. But critics pointed out that he'd actually done precious little to discourage the super-hero image. To be fair, who would have? It was fun and it sold books. Besides, what good did it do to try to discourage it? When he made statements like "I get em-barrassed when people call it courage; I've just done the only thing open to me in the situation,"[2] some took it as false modesty and others as one more example of hero-ism.

Hawking began shouldering, more than previously, the responsibility of being a role model for disabled peo-ple. In a speech before an occupational science confer-ence at the University of Southern California in June 1990 he sounded almost militant. "It is very important that disabled children should be helped to blend with others of the same age. It determines their self-image. How can one feel a member of the human race if one is set apart from an early age. It is a form of apartheid." He said he counts himself lucky that his disease struck him fairly late, after he'd spent his childhood with able-bodied friends, engaged in normal physical games. He praised the mechanical advances that have helped him. But he went on to say that although "aids like wheel-chairs and computers can play an important role in

156

overcoming physical deficiencies, the right mental attitude is even more important. It is no use complaining about the public's attitude about the disabled. It is up to disabled people to change people's awareness in the same way that blacks and women have changed public perceptions."[3] Even Hawking's critics can't deny that he has gone further than almost anyone else in history toward changing that awareness.

While Hawking ranged all over the world giving talks, receiving honors, holding press conferences, and enjoying the general adulation, Cambridge friends watched their "resident supercelebrity" with indulgence and delight, but also with mounting concern. They grudged him none of the fun, but they worried about him. Was he beginning to believe the "master of the universe" image? Would celebrity crowd out his scientific work? Mixed with his usual stubbornness, was it making him a willful prima donna? How would it affect his family? Would the marriage that had survived so much adversity be able to survive this very different threat? The public likes to own its heroes. Could Stephen ever be just Stephen again? It seemed unlikely.

Jane Hawking had sounded an ominous note in an interview in 1989: "I started with great optimism. Stephen was then infected with that optimism. His determination has now rather outstripped mine. I cannot keep up with him. I do think he tends to overcompensate for his condition by doing absolutely everything that comes to his notice."[4] That "everything" had grown out of all proportion. Jane Hawking felt it was a tremendous victory that he was able to live at home and have a fairly normal life. Stephen Hawking wanted much more. There were more doors open to him, more possibilities, than he had ever dreamed of or could ever hope to explore; more demands on his time than he could ever hope to meet. He found it difficult to say no to anything that came along.

157

All these activities and the adulation and awards were distancing him from Jane Hawking and their children. Increasingly they were carving out lives of their own, separate from his. Robert and Lucy were actively trying to be independent and move out of his shadow. Jane Hawking accompanied him less often in his travels. She sought escape in her teaching and her garden and in books and music—as a member of a top-flight Cambridge choir and as a soprano soloist—and with friends who shared her religious faith. Her role in Stephen Hawking's life had changed. It was, she said, no longer to encourage a sick husband. It was "simply to tell him that he's not God."[5]

For twenty-five years Stephen and Jane Hawking together seemed to have handled adversity magnificently. Again and again Stephen Hawking had spoken of their relationship as the mainstay of his life and his success. The "Master of the Universe" television special in 1989 ended with a picture of the two of them watching their sleeping child, Tim, and Hawking's saying, "One really can't ask for more." Life on the edge of the precipice seemed, for all its problems, a beautiful life.

In the spring of 1990 the precipice crumbled in a way very few people had ever expected it would. Just short of their twenty-fifth wedding anniversary the Hawkings separated. Except for a brief mention to the press in the autumn of 1990 that he had left his wife but did not rule out the possibility of a reconciliation, neither Stephen nor Jane Hawking has made any public statement about their separation. It would be inappropriate for us to discuss it in detail here or attempt to explain it. It's symptomatic of the love and respect Hawking's friends and colleagues have for him that in a town where gossip moves like wildfire the news was very slow in spreading. As it did, a widening circle of acquaintances in Cambridge and all over the world reacted to it as a tragedy. It is true that the disintegration

158

of marriages is ordinary and commonplace in today's world, but Hawking and the Hawking marriage had seemed so very un-ordinary.

Hawking no longer has one of the pillars he's always said supported his life: his family. Is another such pillar, his scientific work, also in danger of collapse?

The Lucasian Lecture—Revisited

Stephen Hawking continues to express his devotion to his science. He says he's "itching to get on with it." Is it still possible that he might be the physicist to fit it all together in the Theory of Everything, as the media would have us believe?

Some point out that Hawking's work isn't in the current mainstream of that effort: superstring theory. However, mainstreams in physics shift overnight, and a mind somewhat set apart may spot the connection that makes several streams converge into one complete theory. Others say that by theoretical physics standards Hawking is already well over the hill. It's young people who usually make the great discoveries. A freshness of mind is required, a passionate, brash approach mixed with a certain amount of naïveté. But Hawking certainly still has all of that. It would be a profound mistake to rule him out on those grounds.

Will he live long enough? His illness is still progressing but very slowly. Does he worry about dying before he finishes his work? He answers that he never looks that far ahead. He's lived with the possibility of imminent death for so long that he isn't afraid of it. The kind of work he does is a joint effort, and there are plenty of other physicists to carry on with it. He's never claimed his presence is necessary for the Theory of Everything to be found. "But I'm in no hurry to die," he adds. "There's a lot I want to do first."[6]

In June 1990 I asked Stephen Hawking how he

159

would change his Lucasian lecture of ten years before, were he to write it over again today. *Is* the end in sight for theoretical physics? Yes, he said; he thinks it is. But not by the end of the century. The most promising candidate to unify the forces and particles is no longer the N = 8 supergravity he spoke of then. It's superstrings, the theory that explains the fundamental objects of the universe as tiny, vibrating strings rather than pointlike particles. Superstrings will take a little longer to work out. Give it twenty or twenty-five years.

I asked him whether he believes his no-boundary proposal might turn out to answer the question, What are the boundary conditions of the universe? He answered yes.

He thinks wormhole theory has important implications for a Theory of Everything. Probably, because of wormholes, neither superstrings nor any other theory will be able to predict such fundamental numbers in the universe as particle charges and masses.

And if somebody does find the Theory of Everything, what then? According to Hawking, doing physics after that would be like mountaineering after Mount Everest has been conquered. However, Hawking has also said that for humanity as a whole it would be only the beginning, because although a Theory of Everything would tell us how the universe works and why it is the way it is, it won't tell us why it exists at all. It would be just a set of rules and equations. As we noted before, he wonders, "What is it that breathes fire into the equations and makes a universe for them to describe?" "Why does the universe go to all the bother of existing?"[7] That question, he says, is one that the usual scientific approach of coming up with mathematical models cannot answer.

It's a question not just for scientists but for everybody. Hawking wants to know the answer. "If I knew that, then I would know everything important."[8] As he concludes *A Brief History of Time*, "then we would know the mind of God."[9] But he told a television interviewer, "I'm not so optimistic about finding why the universe exists."[10] He doesn't consider the question of whether we necessarily need to find the Theory of Everything in order to know the mind of God, whether there are, as Jane Hawking suggests, other ways to know God besides in the laws of science.

Meanwhile in the office on Silver Street the small clicking sounds go on and on, the words flit back and forth, up and down, on the computer screen. The synthetic voice enunciates them politely. Students, nurses, and colleagues pass in and out. Every weekday at 4:00 the cups are lined up as precisely as a toy army on the counter in the common room. Former Lucasian Professors of Mathematics gaze down from their portraits on the intent little "rock group on a bad day" as they sip tea and talk their strange mathematical language. The figure in their midst is pitiful by all normal standards, like one of the effigies English children make from rags and cast-off clothes to throw on bonfires on Guy Fawkes night. He wears a bib, and a nurse holds his forehead and tips his head forward so that he can drink his tea out of the cup she holds under his chin. His hair is tousled, his mouth is slack, and his eyes are weary over the eyeglasses that have slipped down his nose a little. But at a disrespectful quip from one of the students his face breaks into a grin that would light the universe.

Whatever the future brings in this unlikely, paradoxical story, we can hope it will be that grin an artist will capture someday in Hawking's portrait, the portrait that will hang in the empty space still remaining on the common room wall beside his office door. Meanwhile the little plaque is a liar. The boss is not asleep.

Source Notes

Chapter 2
1. Richard Feynman, *QED: The Strange Theory of Light and Matter* (Princeton: Princeton University Press, 1985), 4.
2. Stephen W. Hawking, *A Brief History of Time: From the Big Bang to Black Holes* (New York: Bantam, 1988), 9.
3. Ibid.
4. "Professor Hawking's Universe," BBC broadcast, 1983.
5. Hawking, *Brief History of Time*, 174.
6. John A. Wheeler, unpublished poem.
7. Feynman, *QED*, 128.
8. The advertising slogan for the game Othello is "A minute to learn, a lifetime to master."
9. Stephen W. Hawking, "Is the End in Sight for Theoretical Physics?" inaugural lecture as Lucasian Professor of Mathematics, April 1980.
10. Stephen W. Hawking, "Is Everything Determined?" unpublished, 1990.
11. Bryan Appleyard, "Master of the Universe: Will Stephen Hawking Live to Find the Secret?" *Express-News* (San Antonio, Texas), July 3, 1988.
12. Murray Gell-Mann, lecture.

Chapter 3

1. Except where otherwise noted, all quotes in Chapter 3 come from two unpublished articles by Stephen Hawking, "A Short History" and "My Experience with Motor Neurone Disease."
2. Michael Harwood, "The Universe and Dr. Hawking," *New York Times Magazine*, Jan. 23, 1983, 57.
3. Ibid.
4. Ibid.
5. Ibid.
6. "Master of the Universe: Stephen Hawking," BBC broadcast, 1989.
7. Stephen W. Hawking, *A Brief History of Time: From the Big Bang to Black Holes* (New York: Bantam, 1988), 49.
8. Jane Hawking, personal interview, Cambridge, England, April 1991.
9. Bryan Appleyard, "Master of the Universe: Will Stephen Hawking Live to Find the Secret?" *Express-News* (San Antonio, Texas), July 3, 1988.
10. ABC "20/20" broadcast, 1989.

Chapter 4

1. Stephen W. Hawking, "A Short History," unpublished, 5.
2. ABC "20/20" broadcast, 1989.
3. Bob Sipchen, "The Sky No Limit in the Career of Stephen Hawking," *The West Australian* (Perth), June 16, 1990.
4. Bryan Appleyard, "Master of the Universe: Will Stephen Hawking Live to Find the Secret?" *Express-News* (San Antonio, Texas), July 3, 1988.
5. John Boslough, *Beyond the Black Hole: Stephen Hawking's Universe* (Glasgow, Scotland: Fontana/Collins, 1984), 107.
6. Stephen W. Hawking, *A Brief History of Time: From the Big Bang to Black Holes* (New York: Bantam, 1988), 34.
7. Bryce S. DeWitt, "Quantum Gravity," *Scientific American*, 249, #6, Dec. 1983, 114.
8. Hawking, *Brief History of Time*, 42.
9. Stephen W. Hawking (Ph.D. thesis).

Chapter 5

1. Stephen W. Hawking, *A Brief History of Time: From the Big Bang to Black Holes* (New York: Bantam, 1988), 99.

2. Ibid., 105.
3. Stephen Hawking, personal interview, Cambridge, England, December 1989.
4. Hawking, *Brief History of Time*, 108.
5. John Boslough, *Beyond the Black Hole: Stephen Hawking's Universe* (Glasgow, Scotland: Fontana/Collins, 1984), 70.
6. Ibid., 60.
7. Ibid., 70.
8. Ellen Walton, "Brief History of Hard Times" (interview with Jane Hawking), *The Guardian* (London and Manchester, England), Aug. 9, 1989.
9. "Master of the Universe: Stephen Hawking," BBC broadcast, 1989.
10. ABC "20/20" broadcast, 1989.
11. Michael Harwood, "The Universe and Dr. Hawking," *New York Times Magazine*, Jan. 23, 1983, 53.
12. "Master of the Universe: Stephen Hawking," BBC broadcast, 1989.
13. Hawking has said, "If it isn't a black hole, it's really something exotic!"
14. "Master of the Universe: Stephen Hawking."
15. Bryan Appleyard, "Master of the Universe: Will Stephen Hawking Live to Find the Secret?" *Express-News* (San Antonio, Texas), July 3, 1988.
16. Ibid.
17. "Master of the Universe: Stephen Hawking."

Chapter 6
1. Ellen Walton, "Brief History of Hard Times" (interview with Jane Hawking), *The Guardian* (London and Manchester, England), Aug. 9, 1989.
2. Ibid.
3. Ibid.
4. "Master of the Universe: Stephen Hawking," BBC broadcast, 1989.
5. Jane Hawking, personal interview, Cambridge, England, April 1991.
6. Ibid.
7. Michael Harwood, "The Universe and Dr. Hawking," *New York Times Magazine*, Jan. 23, 1983, 58.

8. Ibid., 19.
9. John Boslough, *Beyond the Black Hole: Stephen Hawking's Universe* (Glasgow, Scotland: Fontana/Collins, 1984), 100.
10. Ibid., 101.
11. Ibid., 105.
12. Stephen W. Hawking, *A Brief History of Time: From the Big Bang to Black Holes* (New York: Bantam, 1988), 133.

Chapter 7
1. Stephen W. Hawking, "The Edge of Spacetime," in Paul C. W. Davies, *The New Physics* (Cambridge, England: Cambridge University Press, 1989), 67.
2. Ibid.
3. Ibid., 68.
4. Ibid.
5. Ibid.
6. Jerry Adler, Gerald Lubenow, and Maggie Malone, "Reading God's Mind," *Newsweek*, June 13, 1988, 59.
7. Stephen W. Hawking, "A Short History," unpublished, 6.
8. "Master of the Universe: Stephen Hawking," BBC broadcast, 1989.
9. Don N. Page, "Hawking's Timely Story," *Nature* 332, Apr. 21, 1988, 743.
10. Stephen W. Hawking, *A Brief History of Time: From the Big Bang to Black Holes* (New York: Bantam, 1988), 174.
11. Ibid., 175.

Chapter 8
1. Stephen W. Hawking, "A Brief History of *A Brief History*," *Popular Science*, Aug. 1989, 70.
2. Ellen Walton, "Brief History of Hard Times" (interview with Jane Hawking), *The Guardian* (London and Manchester, England), Aug. 9, 1989.
3. Ibid.
4. Ibid.
5. Stephen W. Hawking, "My Experience with Motor Neurone Disease," unpublished, 1.
6. Hawking, *Brief History of Time*, viii.
7. Hawking, "Brief History of *A Brief History*," 72.

8. Ibid.
9. ABC "20/20" broadcast, 1989.

Chapter 9
1. Ellen Walton, "Brief History of Hard Times" (interview with Jane Hawking), *The Guardian* (London and Manchester, England), Aug. 9, 1989.
2. ABC "20/20" broadcast, 1989.
3. Ibid.
4. Ibid., and "Master of the Universe: Stephen Hawking," BBC broadcast, 1989.
5. ABC "20/20" broadcast.
6. Walton, "Brief History of Hard Times."
7. ABC "20/20" broadcast, 1989.
8. Stephen Hawking, personal interview, Cambridge, England, December 1989.
9. Ibid.
10. Ibid.
11. David H. Freedman, "Maker of Worlds," *Discover*, July 1990, 49.
12. M. Mitchell Waldrop, "The Quantum Wave Function of the Universe," *Science*, 242, Dec. 2, 1988, 1248.
13. Stephen Hawking, personal interview, Cambridge, England, June 1990.
14. Stephen W. Hawking, "Black Holes and Their Children, Baby Universes," unpublished, 7.
15. Ibid., 6.

Chapter 10
1. Dennis Overbye, "The Wizard of Space and Time," *Omni*, February 1979, 45.
2. ABC "20/20" broadcast, 1989.
3. Bob Sipchen, "The Sky No Limit in the Career of Stephen Hawking," *The West Australian* (Perth), June 16, 1990.
4. "Master of the Universe: Stephen Hawking," BBC broadcast, 1989.
5. Bryan Appleyard, "Master of the Universe: Will Stephen Hawking Live to Find the Secret?" *Express-News* (San Antonio, Texas), July 3, 1988.
6. Sipchen, "The Sky No Limit in the Career of Stephen Hawking."

7. Stephen W. Hawking, *A Brief History of Time: From the Big Bang to Black Holes* (New York: Bantam, 1988), 174.
8. M. Mitchell Waldrop, "The Quantum Wave Function of the Universe," *Science*, 242, Dec. 2, 1988, 1250.
9. Hawking, *Brief History of Time*, 175.
10. "Master of the Universe: Stephen Hawking."

Glossary

Antimatter—Matter consisting of antiparticles.

Antiparticle—For every type of particle there exists an antiparticle with opposite properties, such as the sign of its electrical charge (for example, the electron has negative electrical charge; the antielectron, or positron, has positive electrical charge), and other qualities that we haven't dealt with in this book. However, the antiparticles of photons and gravitons are the same as the particles.

Arbitrary element—Something which isn't predicted in a theory but must be learned from observation. For example, an alien who had never seen our universe couldn't take any theory we have so far and figure out from it what the masses and charges are of the elementary particles. These are arbitrary elements in the theories.

Big Bang theory—The theory which says that the universe began in a state of enormous density and pressure and exploded outward and expanded until it is as we see it today.

Big Bang singularity—A singularity at the beginning of the universe.

Black hole—A region of spacetime shaped like a sphere (or a slightly bulged-out sphere in the case of a rotating black hole) which cannot be seen by distant observers because gravity there is so strong that no light (or anything else) can escape from it. Black holes may form from the collapse of massive stars. This was the "classical" definition of a black hole. Hawking showed that a black hole does radiate energy and may not be entirely "black." (Also see **Primordial black hole.**)

Boson—Particle with spin expressed in whole numbers. The messenger particles of the forces (gluons, W^+, W^-, Z°, photons, and gravitons) are bosons.

Boundary conditions—What the universe was like at the instant of beginning, before any time whatsoever had passed. Also what it is like at any other "edge" of the universe—the end of the universe, for example, or the center of a black hole.

Conservation of energy—The law of science that says that energy (or its equivalent in mass) cannot be either created or destroyed.

Cosmological constant—Albert Einstein introduced a "cosmological constant," to counteract gravity, into his theory of general relativity. Without it, the theory predicted that the universe ought to be either expanding or collapsing, neither of which Einstein believed to be true. He later called it "the greatest blunder of my life." We now use the term to mean the energy density of the vacuum.

Cosmology—The study of the very large and of the universe as a whole.

Einstein's general theory of relativity (1915)—The theory of gravity in which gravity is explained as a curvature in four-dimensional spacetime caused by the presence of mass or energy. It provides a set of equations that determines how much curvature is generated by any given distribution of mass or energy. It is a theory that we use to describe gravity at the level of the very large.

Einstein's special theory of relativity (1905)—Einstein's new view of space and time. The theory is based on the idea that the laws of science should be the same for all freely moving observers, no matter what their speed. The speed of light remains unchanged, no matter what the velocity of the observer measuring it is.

Electromagnetic force—One of the four fundamental forces of nature. It causes electrons to orbit the nuclei of atoms. At our level it shows up as light and as all other electromagnetic radiation, such as radio waves, microwaves, X rays, and gamma rays. The messenger particle (boson) of the electromagnetic force is the photon.

Electromagnetic interaction—The interaction in which an electron emits a photon and another electron absorbs it.

Electromagnetic radiation—All forms of radiation that make up the electromagnetic spectrum, such as radio waves, microwaves, visible light, X rays, and gamma rays. All electromagnetic radiation is made up of photons.

Electroweak theory—A theory developed in the 1960s by Abdus Salam at Imperial College, London, and Steven Weinberg and Sheldon Glashow at Harvard, which unified the electromagnetic force and the weak force.

Elementary particle—A particle that we believe is not made up of anything smaller and that cannot be divided.

Entropy—The measurement of the amount of disorder in a system. The second law of thermodynamics

170

states that entropy always increases, never decreases. The universe as a whole, or any isolated system, can never become more orderly.

Escape velocity—The speed necessary to escape the gravity of a massive body such as the earth and escape to elsewhere in space. Escape velocity for the earth is about 7 miles (11 kilometers) per second. Escape velocity for a black hole is slightly greater than the speed of light.

Event—A point in spacetime, specified by its position in time and space, as on a spacetime diagram.

Event horizon—The boundary of a black hole; the radius where escape velocity becomes greater than the speed of light. It is marked by hovering photons, which (moving at the speed of light) cannot escape and also cannot be drawn into the black hole. Light emitted inside it is drawn down into the black hole. *To calculate the radius at which the event horizon forms,* multiply the solar mass of the black hole (the same as for the star that collapsed to form it, unless that star lost mass earlier in the collapse) by 2 for miles or 3 for kilometers. Thus, a 10-solar-mass black hole has its event horizon at a radius of 20 miles or 30 kilometers. You can see that if the mass changes, the radius where the event horizon is will also change, and the black hole will change in size.

Fermion—For the purposes of this book you need to know that particles of ordinary matter (the particles in an atom, such as electrons, neutrons, and protons) belong to a class of particles called fermions, and, like all fermions, they exchange messenger particles. A more technical definition of a fermion is a particle with half-integer spin which obeys the Pauli exclusion principle. We have not dealt with spin or the exclusion principle in this book.

Forces of Nature—The four basic ways that particles

171

can interact with one another. They are, in order from strongest to weakest, the strong force, the weak force, the electromagnetic force, and the gravitational force.

Gamma rays—Electromagnetic radiation of very short wavelengths.

Gluon—The messenger particle which carries the strong force from one quark to another and causes the quarks to hold together in protons and neutrons in the nucleus of the atom. Gluons also interact with one another.

Gravitational force—One of the four fundamental forces of nature, and also the weakest. Gravity always attracts, never repels, and can work over extremely long distances.

Gravitational radius—Photons cannot escape from a black hole to the outside universe from within this radius. You can think of it in the same way as the event horizon, though the two terms are used differently. To figure roughly what this radius will be, multiply the solar mass of the black hole by 2 for miles or 3 for kilometers. Thus a 10-solar-mass black hole will have a radius of 20 miles or 30 kilometers.

Graviton—The messenger particle which carries the gravitational force among all particles in the universe, including gravitons themselves. None has ever been directly observed.

Gravity—*See* **gravitational force.**

Hawking radiation—Radiation produced by a black hole when quantum effects are taken into account. You can think of it as a type of virtual particle pair production near the event horizon of a black hole in which one of the two falls into the hole, allowing the other to escape into space.

Helium—The second lightest of the chemical elements.

The nucleus of a helium atom contains two protons and either one or two neutrons. There are two electrons orbiting the nucleus.

Hydrogen—The lightest of the chemical elements. The nucleus of ordinary hydrogen consists of just one proton. There is a single electron orbiting the nucleus. Hydrogen is fused into helium in the cores of stars.

Imaginary numbers—Numbers that when squared give a negative result. Thus, the square of imaginary two is minus four. The square root of minus nine is imaginary three.

Imaginary time—Time measured using imaginary numbers.

Inflationary universe model—Model in which the early universe went through a short period of extremely rapid expansion.

Initial conditions—The boundary conditions at the beginning of the universe, before any time whatsoever had passed.

Microwave radiation—Electromagnetic radiation that has wavelengths longer than those of visible light and shorter than radio waves. The particles of microwave radiation, as of all radiation in the electromagnetic spectrum, are photons. A background of microwave radiation that we detect in the universe is evidence used to support the idea of the Big Bang model.

N = 8 supergravity—A theory that attempts to unify all the particles, both bosons and fermions, in a supersymmetric family, and to unify the forces. This was the theory Hawking spoke of in his 1980 Lucasian lecture and which he thought might turn out to be the Theory of Everything.

Neutron—One of the particles that make up the nucleus of an atom. Neutrons have no electric charge. Every neutron is made up of three smaller particles called quarks.

Newton's theory of gravity—Each body in the universe is attracted toward every other by a force that is stronger the more massive the bodies are and the closer they are to one another. Stated more precisely: Bodies attract each other with a force that is proportional to their mass and inversely proportional to the square of the distance between them.

No-boundary proposal—The idea that the universe is finite but has no boundary (in imaginary time).

Nucleus—The central part of an atom, made up of protons and neutrons (which in turn are made up of quarks). The nucleus is held together by the strong force.

Particle pairs—Pairs of particles that are being created everywhere in the vacuum and all the time. They are usually thought to be virtual particles, are extremely short-lived, and cannot be detected except indirectly by observing their effect on other particles. In a fraction of a second the two particles in a pair must find each other again and annihilate one another.

Photon—The messenger particle of the electromagnetic force. At our level, photons show up as visible light and as all the other radiation in the electromagnetic spectrum, such as radio waves, microwaves, X rays, and gamma rays. Photons have zero mass and move at the speed of light.

Positron—Antiparticle of the electron. It has positive electric charge.

Primordial black hole—Tiny black hole created not by the collapse of a star but the pressing together of matter in the very early universe. According to Hawking the most interesting ones are about the size of the nucleus of an atom, with a mass of about a billion tons.

Proton—One of the particles that make up the nucleus of the atom. Protons have a positive electric charge. Every proton is made up of three smaller particles called quarks.

Pulsar—A neutron star that rotates very rapidly and sends out regular pulses of radio waves, sometimes several hundred to a thousand times a second.

Quantum fluctuations—The constant appearance and disappearance of virtual particles that occur in what we think of as empty space (the vacuum).

Quantum mechanics or quantum theory—The theory developed in the 1920s that we use to describe the very small, generally things the size of the atom and smaller. According to the theory, light, X rays, and any other waves can only be emitted or absorbed in certain "packages" called quanta. For instance, light occurs in quanta known as photons, and it can't be divided up into smaller "packages" than one photon. You can't have half a photon, for example, or one and three-quarters photons. In quantum theory energy is said to be "quantized." The theory includes the uncertainty principle.

Quantum wormhole (*See* **wormhole**.)—A wormhole of an unimaginably small size.

Quarks—The fundamental particles (meaning they can't be divided into anything smaller), which, banded together in groups of three, make up protons and neutrons. Quarks also band together in groups of two (one quark and one antiquark) to form particles called mesons.

Radio waves—Electromagnetic waves with longer wavelengths than those of visible light. The particles of radio waves, as of all radiation in the electromagnetic spectrum, are photons.

Radioactivity—The spontaneous breakdown of one type of atomic nucleus into another.

Radius—The shortest distance from the center of a circle or sphere to the circumference or surface.

Renormalization—A process that is used to remove infinities from a theory. It involves putting in other infinities and allowing the infinities to cancel one another out.

Second law of thermodynamics—Entropy, the amount of disorder, in an isolated system can only increase, never decrease. If two systems join, the entropy of the combined system is as great as or greater than the entropy of the two systems added together.

Singularity—A point in spacetime at which spacetime curvature becomes infinite, a point of infinite density. Some theories predict that we will find a singularity at the center of a black hole or at the beginning or end of the universe.

Solar mass—Mass equaling the mass of our sun.

Spacetime—The combination of the three dimensions of space and one dimension of time.

Spacetime curvature—Einstein's theory of general relativity explains the force of gravity as the way the distribution of mass or energy in spacetime causes something that resembles the warping, denting, and dimpling in an elastic surface by heavy pellets of different weights and sizes lying on it.

Strong force—The strongest of the four fundamental forces of nature. It holds the quarks together, in neutrons and protons for instance, and is responsible for the way protons and neutrons hold together in the nucleus. The messenger particle (boson) of the strong force is the gluon.

Supernova—An enormous explosion of a star in which all but the inner core is blown off into space. The material blown off in a supernova forms the raw material for new stars and for planets.

Superstring theory—The theory that explains the fundamental objects in the universe not as pointlike particles but as tiny strings or loops of string. It is a leading candidate for unifying all the particles and forces.

Theory of Everything—Sometimes called the T.O.E., this is the nickname for the theory that explains the universe and everything that happens in it.

Uncertainty principle—A particle cannot have both a definite position and a definite velocity at the same time. The more precisely you measure the one, the less accurate your measurement of the other will be. Similarly you cannot measure precisely the value of a field and its rate of change over time. There are other pairs of quantities that present the same problem. The uncertainty principle was discovered by the German physicist Werner Heisenberg and is more properly called the Heisenberg uncertainty principle.

Unified theory—A theory that explains all four forces as one "superforce" showing up in different ways and that also unites both fermions and bosons in a single family.

Velocity—The speed at which something is moving away from some fixed place, and the direction in which it is moving.

Virtual particle—In quantum mechanics a particle that can never be directly detected, but whose existence we know about because we can measure its effect on other particles.

W^+, W^-, Z°—The messenger particles (bosons) of the weak force.

Weak force—One of the four fundamental forces of nature. The messenger particles (bosons) of the weak force are the W^+, W^-, and the $Z°$. The weak force is responsible for radioactivity, such as a type called beta radioactivity in the nuclei of atoms.

Wormhole—A hole or tunnel in spacetime, which may end in another universe or another part (or time) of our own universe.

Bibliography

(Those marked with an asterisk are recommended for further reading at a level similar to this book.)

"A Brief History." *The New Yorker,* Apr. 18, 1988, 30–31.

Abbott, Larry F. "Baby Universes and Making the Cosmological Constant Zero." *Nature,* 336, Dec. 22, 29, 1988, 711–12.

Adler, Jerry, Gerald Lubenow, and Maggie Malone. "Reading God's Mind." *Newsweek,* June 13, 1988, 56–59.

Appleyard, Bryan. "Master of the Universe: Will Stephen Hawking Live to Find the Secret?" *Express-News* (San Antonio, Texas), July 3, 1988.

Barnett, Stephen M. "Photons Faster than Light?" *Nature,* 344, Mar. 22, 1990, 289.

Bartusiak, Marcia. "What Place for a Creator?" *New York Times Book Review,* Apr. 3, 1988, 10–11.

*Boslough, John. *Beyond the Black Hole: Stephen Hawking's Universe.* Glasgow, Scotland: Fontana/Collins, 1984.

———. "Inside the Mind of a Genius." *Reader's Digest,* February 1984, 119–23.

Catoir, Father John. "Power behind Creation." *The Beacon,* Mar. 22, 1990, 17.

*Chaisson, Eric. *Relatively Speaking: Relativity, Black Holes, and the Fate of the Universe.* New York: W. W. Norton & Co., 1988.

Coleman, Sidney. Telephone interview with author. July 1990.

*Davies, Paul C. W. *God and the New Physics.* New York: Viking Penguin, 1983.

*———. "The New Physics: A Synthesis." In *The New Physics,* edited by Paul C. W. Davies. Cambridge, England: Cambridge University Press, 1989.

*DeWitt, Bryce S. "Quantum Gravity." *Scientific American,* 249, #6, December 1983, 112–29.

———. Telephone interview with author. September 1990.

Dodd, James E. *The Ideas of Particle Physics: An Introduction for Scientists.* Cambridge, England: Cambridge University Press, 1984. (Reprinted with corrections, 1988.)

*Feynmann, Richard P. *QED: The Strange Theory of Light and Matter.* Princeton: Princeton University Press, 1985.

Freedman, Daniel Z., and Peter van Nieuwenhuizen. "Supergravity and the Unification of the Laws of Physics." *Scientific American,* February 1978, 226–43.

*Freedman, David H. "Maker of Worlds." *Discover*, July 1990, 46–52.

Friedman, John L. "Back to the Future." *Nature*, 336, Nov. 24, 1988, 305–6.

*Gribbin, John. *In Search of the Big Bang*. London: Corgi Books, 1986.

Halpern, Jules P. "Black Holes in the Balance." *Nature*, 344, Apr. 19, 1990, 713–14.

Harwood, Michael. "The Universe and Dr. Hawking." *The New York Times Magazine*, Jan. 23, 1983, 16–19.

Hawking, Stephen W. "A Brief History of *A Brief History*." *Popular Science*, August 1989, 70–72.

*———. *A Brief History of Time: From the Big Bang to Black Holes*. New York: Bantam, 1988.

———. "A Short History." Unpublished. N.d.

———. "Baby Universes II." *Modern Physics Letters* A, 5, 7, 1990, 453–66.

———. "Black Holes and Their Children, Baby Universes." Unpublished. N.d.

*———. "The Edge of Spacetime." in *The New Physics*, edited by Paul C. W. Davies. Cambridge, England: Cambridge University Press, 1989.

———. Interviews with author. Cambridge, England, December 1989 and June 1990.

———. "Is Everything Determined?" Unpublished, 1990.

———. "Is the End in Sight for Theoretical Physics?" Inaugural lecture as Lucasian Professor of Mathematics, April 1980.

———. "My Experience with Motor Neurone Disease." Unpublished. N.d.

*———. "The Quantum Mechanics of Black Holes." *Scientific American*, January 1977, 34–40.

———. "Wormholes in Spacetime." Unpublished. August 1987.

Isham, Chris. "Quantum Gravity." In *The New Physics*, edited by Paul C. W. Davies. Cambridge, England: Cambridge University Press, 1989.

Jaroff, Leon. "Roaming the Cosmos." *Time*, Feb. 8, 1988, 58–60.

*Longair, Malcolm. "The New Astrophysics." In *The New Physics*, edited by Paul C. W. Davies. Cambridge, England: Cambridge University Press, 1989.

Maddox, John. "The Big *Big Bang* Book." *Nature*, 336, Nov. 17, 1988, 267.

"Master of the Universe: Stephen Hawking." BBC broadcast, 1989.

Misner, Charles W., Kip S. Thorne, and John Archibald Wheeler. *Gravitation*. San Francisco: W. H. Freeman & Co., 1970.

Morais, Richard C. "Genius Unbound." *Forbes*, Mar. 23, 1987, 142.

Moss, Ian. "A SQUID's Loss of Coherence." *Nature*, 343, Feb. 8, 1990, 515.

———. "Wormholes in Space-time." *Nature*, 330, Nov. 19, 1987, 210.

Overbye, Dennis. "The Wizard of Space and Time." *Omni*, February 1979, 45–107.

Page, Don N. "Hawking's Timely Story." *Nature*, 332, Apr. 21, 1988, 742–43.

"Professor Hawking's Universe." BBC broadcast, 1983.

Rogers, Tony. "Stephen Hawking: A Man and His Universe." *Richmond Times-Dispatch,* June 10, 1990.

Salam, Abdus. "Overview of Particle Physics." In *The New Physics,* edited by Paul C. W. Davies, Cambridge, England: Cambridge University Press, 1989.

Siegel, Matthew. "Wolf Foundation Honors Hawking and Penrose for Work on Relativity." *Physics Today,* January 1989, 97–98.

Sipchen, Bob. "The Sky No Limit in the Career of Stephen Hawking." *The West Australian* (Perth), June 16, 1990.

Starobinskii, A. A., and Ya. B. Zel'dovich. "Quantum Effects in Cosmology." *Nature,* 331, Feb. 25, 1988, 673–74.

"Stephen Hawking—Mastering the Universe." ABC News "20/20" broadcast, 1989.

*Waldrop, M. Mitchell. "The Quantum Wave Function of the Universe." *Science,* 242, Dec. 2, 1988, 1248–50.

Walton, Ellen. "Brief History of Hard Times." *The Guardian* (London and Manchester, England), Aug. 9, 1989.

Wheeler, John Archibald. "Behind It All." Unpublished poem.

———. Interview with author. Hightstown, N.J., and New York, N.Y., June 1989.

*———. *Journey into Gravity and Spacetime.* New York: W. H. Freeman, 1990.

*Will, Clifford. "The Renaissance of General Relativity." In *The New Physics,* edited by Paul C. W. Davies. Cambridge, England: Cambridge University Press, 1989.

Index

Insert references indicate illustrations.

188

scientific theory and, 18–20

success and, 132–135, 137–139, 155–158

sums-over-histories and, 107, 110

superstring theory and, 149, 160

Theory of Every-thing and, 11, 21, 22, 29–30, 76, 145, 149, 159–161

wife and, 48, 50, 84–86, 88–92, 126–127, 157–159

wormholes and, 139, 141, 142, 144–145, 147–148, 160

See insert

Hawking, Tim, 89, 129, 132, 136, 155, 158, insert page 10

Hawking radiation, 79, 81, 82, 97, 98, 115, 141, 144, 146

Hodgkin, Sir Alan, 92

Hoyle, Fred, 38, 39, 94

Hubble, Edwin, 50–51, 66, 67

Imaginary numbers, 110, 112

Imaginary time, 110, 112, 118, 123, 141, 148, 150–151

Inflationary expansion, 120

Initial conditions of, universe, 16–17, 20, 23, 119, 160

Institute of Astronomy, England, 48

King's College, London, 45, 83

Kuchar, Karel, 121

Light, 15, 20, 24, 52 speed of, 54–55, 62–63, 79, 112–113

See also Photons

London University, 47, 48

Lou Gehrig's disease, 10, 40, 41

Masey, Sue, 153

Mason, David, 129

Mass, 53, 54, 56, 57, 58, 59, 64, 79, 81, 144–145

"Master of the Universe: Stephen Hawking" (television show), 135, 158

Motor neurone disease, 10, 40, 41

National Health Service (NHS), England, 127, 138

189

National Institute for Medical Research, England, 33

Nature (magazine), 83, 121

N = 8 Supergravity, 11, 160

Neutrons, 15, 26–27

Newsweek (magazine), 135

Newton, Sir Isaac, 10, 14, 19, 21, 25, 53, 54, 56, 57, 79, 85, 92

New York Times, The, 91

No-boundary proposal, 20, 93, 118–123, 148, 160

Nuclei of atoms, 15, 16, 27, 98–99

Oxford University ("Univ"), England, 34–36

Page, Don, 91, 121, insert page 9

Particle pairs, 77–79, 115, 146

Particles, 15–16, 20, 22, 24, 26–27, 29, 51–53, 58, 62, 65, 76–78, 82, 97, 144–145, 147, 150

Penguins, 21

Penrose, Roger, 44, 52, 64, 66, 69, 71, 72

Philip, Prince, 139

Photons, 15, 27, 58, 64, 72–73, 77, 112–113, 144. *See also* Light

Planets, 22, 24, 51–53, 61, 141

Pneumonia, 126

Pressure, 62

Primordial black holes, 81, 97–98, 150

Protons, 15, 26–27

Pulsars, 21

Quantum fluctuations, 116, 117, 145, 148

Quantum mechanics, 22–24, 26–29, 58, 75–78, 83, 97–99, 112–113, 115–116, 117, 123, 140, 144, 148

Quantum variables, 145, 148

Quantum wormholes. *See* Wormholes

Quarks, 27

Quasars, 24

Radiation, 16, 64, 79, 80, 81, 97

Relativity, Einstein's theories of, 20–24, 39, 52, 54–58, 66–67, 71, 76, 83, 97, 99, 100, 107, 146, 148

Religion, 85–86, 93–95, 121–122

Renormalization, 23

Rockefeller Institute, New York, 132
Royal Society, 91–92
Rutherford, Ernest, 10, 27, 28, 98
Rutherford-Appleton Laboratory, England, 82

Saint Alban's School, England, 33, 42, insert page 4
Sciama, Denis, 39, 41, 42, 45, 82, 83
Second law of black hole dynamics, 73, 79
Second law of thermodynamics, 73–74
Shames, Stephen, 136
Sherman Fairchild Distinguished Scholar, 92
Singularities, 44, 66, 69, 71, 93, 96, 98, 120, 122, 123, 148, 150, 151
Solar systems, 94, 95
Spacetime, 65, 100, 102, 103, 104, 105, 107, 108, 110, 118
Spielberg, Stephen, 155
Starobinskii, Alexander, 76
Stars, 22, 24, 51, 52, 58, 61–64, 66, 69, 72–73, 94, 120, 140, 141

Strong force, 16, 27
Sums-over-histories, 105–107, 110
Supergravity, 23, 146
Supernovas, 94
Superstring theory, 19, 23, 149, 159, 160

Theory, scientific, definition of, 17–20
Theory of Everything, 11, 13–14, 16–17, 20–24, 26, 29–30, 71, 76, 145, 149, 159–161
Thomson, "J. J.," 9
Time, 54–55, 68–69, 100, 102, 103, 105, 107, 110, 112, 118
Time (magazine), 131, 133
"20/20" (television show), 135

Uncertainty principle, 22–24, 26, 27, 28, 29, 77, 98–99, 112, 113, 114, 115, 116, 140, 145, 146
University of Bristol, England, 138

V-2 rocket, 33

Weak force, 16, 19, 27
Westfield College, London, 42

191

Wheeler, John
  Archibald, 21, 44, 52,
  95, 117, 139,
Woltosz, Walt, 127
World-lines, 100, 102–
  103, 104, 105, 106,
  107, 110, 113, 116
World War II, 32, 33

Wormholes, 20, 21, 115,
  139, 141, 142, 143,
  144–145, 147–150,
  154, 160
W's, 27

Zel'dovich, Yakov, 76
Z's, 27